THE JOY
— OF —
Pickleball

Also by Mike Branon

Pickleball and the Art of Living
(Three chapters follow the About the Author page.)

THE JOY
— OF —
Pickleball

The Definitive Instructional
Guide for the Senior Player

MIKE BRANON

Black Seal Press   Carlsbad, California

Printed in the United States of America
First Edition, 2022

Published by Black Seal Press
Carlsbad, California

ISBN: 979-8-9863543-0-9 (paperback)
ISBN: 979-8-9863543-1-6 (ebook)

Disclaimer: This book is designed to provide information and motivation to its readers. It is sold with the understanding that the author and publisher are not engaged to render any type of psychological, legal, or any other kind of professional advice. The content of each article is the sole expression and opinion of its author and is not meant to substitute for any advice from your healthcare professionals, lawyers, therapists, business advisors/partners, or personal connections.

Every effort has been made to credit the original source for images in this book. If you feel a photo has been used without permission, please contact info@mikebranon.com.

Publishing services provided by AuthorImprints.com

Contents

CONTENTS

Introduction

WHEN YOU DIVE INTO A NONFIC-tion book, you are seeking to learn or maybe change something in your life. At the very least, you are looking to be entertained or encouraged to think differently than you did before. Understanding the motivation of the author when you make a commitment to read their book is important so you can see if their goals are in alignment with yours. After all, I hope we're about to spend some quality time together.

What do I, the author, want out of this? Am I out to make money or upsell you with other products and services? Do I want to become famous and be seen as an authority in my field? There's nothing wrong with these motivations. Writing a book usually makes no economic sense without these corollary benefits.

However, I can honestly tell you that my motivation is none of the above. I'm about as famous as I want to be, which is not so much. I'm also guessing that my author income is somewhere south of five cents an hour and I'd rather be playing pickleball than raising my social media profile.

My true motivation is to make your life just a little better.

If you play pickleball, you are obviously a wise and wonderful person already, but I want to help you play even better, healthier, and happier. My lifelong interest and experience in sports, health, and psychology has convinced me that an active mind and body are the keys to living well, especially as we age.

Pickleball is the perfect prescription to serve this purpose, keeping us moving and challenging us to learn and strategize without pushing our physical boundaries so far that we end up frustrated or injured. The game also provides another essential ingredient we need—connection. A connected, active, challenging lifestyle is the true Fountain of Youth. It makes life interesting and gives purpose to our days.

I wrote this book specifically with senior players (50+) in mind, but most of the advice I give is suitable for all ages. If you happen to be a youngster in your 30s or 40s, there is plenty in these pages that will help you play your best and enjoy your pickleball experience more. However, in my teaching and coaching career, I have been moved by the desire of older folks to find something that is not only good for them but also inspires them to excel and have fun. The great thing about pickleball is that players over 50 can compete quite well with younger athletes. Unlike football or basketball, you don't need to run a 4.40 forty-yard dash or possess a 42" vertical leap. Pickleball is the perfect mix of movement, skill, and strategy—challenging, but accessible to a wide range of participants. More importantly, it's just plain fun.

I have never heard more laughter during a sporting activity than on a pickleball court, but I have also experienced and seen a lot of frustration. We all want to play our best and can be quite self-judgmental when we don't. How do we thread the needle of challenging ourselves and improving without feeling bad about ourselves in the process?

That is the question I hope to answer with a combination of instruction and advice on how to develop an attitude that makes every day enjoyable, no matter who wins. We all learn in different ways, so I have enhanced my written instruction with videos that clarify key points. And I have included information and stories that are designed to educate and inspire.

Finally, I have attempted to do all this as concisely as possible, so the messages come through clearly. In the world we live in, information overload can overwhelm and confuse us. Simple concepts enable us to play our best, avoid overthinking on the court, and retain what we have learned. Sometimes, less is more.

You now have a clear understanding of my motivations and goals in writing this book. Thank you for coming along. I hope you learn something, have a laugh or two, and realize how fortunate we are to still be able to run around and play like a bunch of kids at recess.

All videos in this book can be viewed at https://www.mikebranon.com/joy

LET'S PLAY!

HUMANS LOVE TO PLAY. It's one of the things that makes life worth living. However, as we get older, our options for playtime can become limited to less demanding pursuits. We do need to make some concessions to age, but for many of us, the fire to compete still burns brightly. We're not ready to make shuffleboard and jigsaw puzzles the most demanding activities we take on, but our bodies may not be able to take the pounding from running, soccer, tennis, and other high-impact sports that we used to love. What to do?

For more and more of us, pickleball has come to the rescue. It can be played at high levels, demanding athleticism and skillful technique. It can also be played recreationally and not as seriously, allowing the less experienced or less mobile player an opportunity to enjoy relaxed competition and have fun while getting some great exercise in the bargain.

No matter where you are on the age and ability spectrum,

you can find a game that suits your needs. You can compete against younger players using guile, finesse, and experience to overcome power and speed. Or you can find folks that just love knocking the ball around, being outside, and having a good time. Because pickleball is relatively easy to learn but difficult to master, it is both accessible and challenging.

If you already play, you know this to be true. If you're new to the game, this book is the appetizer to your pickleball entrée—bite-sized, easy to digest, and a teaser for the main course. You'll soon find out why the rest of us raving lunatics are so passionate about our game.

The purpose of this book is to help you:

- **Play Better**
- **Play Healthier**
- **Play Happier**

Specifically, I want to help the senior player get the most out of their game. There are many books on pickleball, and pickleball instruction in particular. However, this book is dedicated to you, the more mature athlete who may have different priorities than a younger player.

Along the way, I will give you tips on how to play better, healthier, and happier, so you get the most out of your pickleball journey. And I will seek to entertain and motivate you with stories that show how meaningful this sport can be to those of us whose odometers have more than a few miles on them.

I will also focus on the mental and psychological factors

that can make your game more effective and enjoyable. It's a more holistic approach that goes beyond the physical game and encompasses the entire experience of being part of the pickleball community. Every senior player wants to play better and win more games—we're still competitors at heart. But let's be honest... many of us can't remember the scores of the games we played yesterday (I just assume I won and don't bother with any messy facts).

If we're not competing for championships and being interviewed on ESPN, why do we keep showing up at the courts every chance we get? It's the feeling of being with friends, challenging ourselves to improve, and having a hell of a good time.

After extensive research, I noticed that a lot of people I met on the court limped, groaned, and had trouble reading menus. I also found out that there was a ton of pickleball instruction out there but nothing that specifically addressed the needs of the senior player. So, I started tinkering with a book that would be short and to the point—a definitive guide for the senior pickleballer. But what would I call it? *Pickleball For Seniors* was the original working title, but it died of boredom. Then I remembered that racy book from years ago, *The Joy of Sex*, and thought, "What turns seniors on these days? What makes them all sweaty, feel intense passion, and cry out with joy when they do it right? Probably not sex so much anymore. It's got to be pickleball."

That's why this book is called *The Joy of Pickleball*. This joyfulness is found in different aspects of the game. There is the thrill of competing, the kinship of community, and the feeling that you are unleashing your inner All-Star when you play well. In fact, don't let reality get in the way of how you visualize yourself on the court:

HOW YOU SEE YOURSELF:

REALITY:

The Press Democrat, May 15, 2015 (Kent Porter, PD)

When I coach and play with senior athletes, I feel a kinship with people who have experienced a fulfilling life and aren't ready to stop moving, learning, and challenging themselves to be better. They have realized an important lesson—getting older doesn't mean giving up. It's simply time to *reimagine your athletic life*. If that sounds like you, let's dig in and make your pickleball experience the best it can be!

THE HEART OF
THE MATTER

I T'S INSTRUCTIVE AND REVEALING to reduce anything in life to its essentials: *"What is it? How do I do it? And why?"*

Once we understand what it is we are trying to accomplish with utter clarity, our focus sharpens, and we are empowered to learn and excel. However, it's not enough to understand what something is and how to do it right—there must be a compelling "Why" that inspires and gives meaning to the pursuit. It's the "Why" that imbues anything in life with passion and purpose.

The following graphic is my attempt to simplify the game, summarizing key technical concepts and the deeper motivations that compel us to make pickleball part of our lives.

This book will attempt to put some meat on the bare bones of these concepts so that you can enjoy the feast with your friends in your senior years. Refer back to these principles to remain focused on what you're trying to do and why you're doing it in the first place. When you integrate the physical and mental aspects of the game with a keen awareness of why pickleball fits your lifestyle, you will play better, healthier, and happier.

HOW TO PLAY

PHYSICAL
Positioning
Preparation
Footwork
Body/Stroke Mechanics
Paddle Position

MENTAL
Patience
Shot Location
Intention/Shot Selection
Strategy
Teamwork/ Communication

WHY WE PLAY

Challenge
Competition
Connection
Health

Exercise
Personal Growth
Happiness
Purpose

But first, let's set the stage. Why has pickleball become so popular? And why has the sport continued to boom among senior players in particular?

A GAME BUILT FOR US

PICKLEBALL HAS CHANGED LIVES and expanded horizons for many people. Pickleball is for everyone, but it's *really* tailor-made for seniors who long for competition and connection, seeking to reawaken their passion for sports from younger days.

The numbers don't lie: *

- Pickleball grew in 2021 to 4.8 million players in the US, an incredible growth rate of 39.3% in two years.
- 60% of core players (those who play 8+ times a year) are 55 or older.

Yes, pickleball is exploding in popularity. And there's a good

---

* USA Pickleball 2021 Fact and Media Sheet 1 and SFIA Sports, Fitness & Leisure Activities Topline Participation Report reason—this game can change your life... no magic pills or expensive programs required. Players of all ages are flocking to the sport, but as you can see above, most core players are 55 or older. We may feel more marginalized or invisible as we age, but not on the pickleball court. This is *our* turf (concrete)!

Why does pickleball resonate with our demographic? What does it mean to be an older athlete? How do we embrace our age with a sense of humor and perspective?

> Experience is the hardest kind of teacher.
> It gives you the test first and
> the lesson afterward.
> ~ *Oscar Wilde*

The good news is that what we lack in ability as we age, we make up for in experience. We have been tested often in life and have accumulated a lot of lessons—some the hard way. If only we could remember what those lessons were...

You still have your good days, but when you catch yourself struggling to put on your socks or forgetting why you just walked so purposefully into the kitchen, well, as the saying goes:

> When your mind makes contracts your body can't
> fill.
> You're over the hill, son. You're over the hill.
> ~ *Ram Dass*

We marvel at the vibrancy of youth. Their energy and

physicality are something to behold. On the court, we sometimes think we haven't lost a step when we're playing with friends our age. But when you hit a perfect drop shot, and some darn 25-year-old effortlessly gets to the ball and zips it past you, it's a bit of a reality check.

The crucial question is, "Can we rediscover our power and vigor at any age, or is this the exclusive arena of the young?" The truth, as it usually does, lies somewhere in the middle. Most of us have neither the energy nor the desire to completely reinvent ourselves. That's just fine. We've earned the right to turn down the "stress meter", but we don't want to turn it down too far and end up stagnant and purposeless. Skillful aging demands that we stay involved and invested in our world, or at least our town. We may not be at our peak, but we're still giving it our best shot.

For lifelong athletes, it's natural to glorify past accomplishments and wax nostalgic about the young, vibrant competitors we once were. (It's funny how that homerun you hit in high school went 350 feet when you reminisced about it at your 50th birthday but was miraculously a 400-footer at your 60th. The ball may still be rolling by the time you tell the same story at your 70th!) If you had a favorite sport when you were younger, but your body can no longer handle the demands without risking injury, it's not time to give up. Getting old doesn't mean giving up, it means finding creative ways to stay in the game.

I'm in my 60s but I remember vividly the time many years ago when I received my first senior discount without asking for one and well before I deserved one. (Yes, I took the discount. No need to have my buddy laugh at me *and* pay more than necessary.)

What is a "senior" anyway? To someone younger than 30, it could be someone vaguely 50ish or older. To someone in their 60s, it's those fogeys in their 70s. And to someone in their 70s, it's those octogenarians who are slowing down the buffet line.

What is a "senior" in the pickleball world? In official pickleball competition, senior events are age 50 and above. If you don't play tournaments, you qualify as a senior if you make that groaning noise when you get out of your chair or pick up a ball. In this climate of triggering and political correctness, is it even okay to call someone a "senior"? I recently read that this term is considered offensive to some. They prefer the term, "life-experienced person". I prefer to call old things old, but maybe that's because I'm so crotchety and "life-experienced".

As Einstein would point out, age is relative: *It's not how OLD you are, it's how YOU are.* Your intellectual curiosity and activity level are key to remaining vibrant at any age. I'm always on the lookout for things that make me feel young, active, and connected—anything that stirs my sense of passion and gets me out the door every morning instead of retreating to a comfy chair until it's time for lunch. And that, my friend, is how I found pickleball.

After shredding ankle ligaments, ruining my back, and having my face rearranged one too many times, I moved on from competitive basketball at age 50 and threw myself into golf and tennis—more age-appropriate sports. I still enjoy them, but ever since I randomly wandered upon a group of strangers playing this funky sport and they insisted I join them, pickleball is the thing that checks all my boxes and warms my cockles.*

Take a moment to remember how you discovered pickleball. Chances are it was also some random encounter that sparked your interest. Or maybe it was some pickleball evangelist trumpeting the good word (sometimes a bit too enthusiastically?).

If you are a pickleball veteran, you have probably played the role of ambassador or teacher to friends who want to get into the game. We enjoy our status as a "niche" sport and take pride in growing our community.

A bit of history: In the 70s, the company Pickle-Ball Inc. marketed the tagline, "Say Goodbye to the Sidelines." Since pickleball was new, the idea was to have a saying that shared what the game did—getting people of all ages and skill levels off the sidelines and giving them an opportunity to play. And the folks who invented the game deliberately designed it so their wives, kids, and older friends could compete on a more level playing field. Finesse and tactics were rewarded, enabling less physically gifted players to hold their own.

---

* *Cockles is a variation of the Latin phrase for the heart's ventricles, cochleae cordis. So, yes, even though it sounds potentially inappropriate, it means heartwarming.*

There's a reason why retirement communities are built around golf courses and tennis/pickleball courts instead of basketball courts and football fields. We still want to play and compete, but we have enough doctor's appointments as it is. Many of us still love how alive we feel when we are competing. We just need to be a little smarter about how we do it.

Enter pickleball. . . the Goldilocks of senior sports.

It's not as hard on the body as tennis but it gets the heart revved up more than golf. You may not be able to run like you used to, but you can still move around quite a bit in short bursts on a pickleball court. And walking is great for you, but it's usually not the most social of activities.

As Goldilocks would say, "Pickleball is *just right*."

Even if you are not a natural athlete, you can find a group that fits you. There's nothing wrong with enjoying the game as a beginner and never progressing to higher levels. If you're having fun, getting some exercise, and enjoying your companions, you're winning at pickleball.

You can play at your own level no matter what age you are. You can use the pickleball rating system or my favorite system (common sense) to find players who match up well with your skill and personality. You can set up private games, attend open play, or even enter tournaments if that's what floats your boat.

Finesse can beat power, and as a welcome bonus, the game is relatively inexpensive. You can pay more for that new "miracle" golf club than you would spend playing pickleball for a year. Pickleball also improves hand-eye coordination, balance, and cardiovascular health.* It simply keeps you moving. Remember. . .

The more you move now, the more you move later.

---

* If you're concerned about the health benefits of pickleball versus the risk of injury, before you read any further, skip to Chapter 6 for a more detailed analysis. Suffice to say that older folks running around on concrete and smashing objects at each other is more perilous than a game of Scrabble, but I will offer suggestions on how to stay as healthy as possible when you take up the game. Most of us diehards gladly accept the risks in favor of the many benefits of staying active and engaged.

Best of all, you can meet other active seniors (and even those young whippersnappers under 50), form friendships, and have something to poke fun at each other about at Happy Hour. (Note: the founding fathers of our sport cherished their Happy Hours and trash-talking, so when you do this, you're not being obnoxious, you're keeping their legacy alive!) It's the relationships and camaraderie that we remember long after we have forgotten the scores of the games from last week (or a few minutes ago. . .).*

"Life-experienced" athletes have a home in pickleball. It's a game that's built for us. And it's up to us to continue building it for the generations to come.

---

* One of the funniest and most disconcerting things about this game is that even with experienced players, every now and then, you finish a long point and all four players find themselves staring at each other, trying to remember the score. Eventually, someone figures it out or we just give up and go with our best guess. Good thing we're not playing for money...

THE PICKLEBALL ADDICTION

PICKLEBALL IS ONE OF THE FAST-est-growing sports in the world. What is it that is so addictive about this game? Is it the competition, the amazing social connections, or the ability to enjoy yourself even if you were picked last for kickball back in the day? It's all those things, and much more.

You don't have to be the fastest, most powerful athlete on your block to play the game well. In fact, it's the ability to control and place your shots that make the difference. It's a chess match—you're standing on the board, constructing points, and using fundamentals to checkmate your opponents. It's also almost always a team game. Singles pickleball is rarely played by seniors, and for good reason—it's very challenging to cover so much court area and there's a premium on power and athleticism. But doubles is where the fun is! You learn to play with different partners, using communication and moving together to win points.

Four players in a relatively small area makes for a more intimate feel than with other sports. You're not hammering away from distant baselines as in tennis. If you're where you're supposed to be—at the kitchen line*—then you're 14 feet away from your opponent. This proximity is far enough to be socially distanced but close enough to be socially engaged.

If you close your eyes and listen to pickleball games in progress on multiple courts, you'll hear the constant, staccato "thwack" of paddle on hard plastic ball, but best of all, you'll hear excited shouts, groans, and exclamations. You may even learn a new combination of four-letter words, but most of us picklers are usually quite well-behaved.

However, it's the laughter you will hear that sets pickleball apart. Many other sports can lean toward seriousness. You can definitely find some competitive, hard-core pickleball games, but the general ambiance is usually one of good-natured, mutually supportive activity. It's this cocktail of challenge and connection that explains the love we have for our game.

Your social life becomes much richer when you take up pickleball. Your circle of friends expands, and you look forward to each day that brings you activity, competition, and

---

* For you newbies, the kitchen line isn't where you wait for the waffle maker at the La Quinta Inn. It's the forward zone of the court in which you cannot volley. More on this later.

THE JOY OF PICKLEBALL

new relationships on and off the court. As we age, we need connection with others more than ever. Our changing world has seen an explosion of online connection, but it often comes at the expense of real human interaction. Pickleball puts you side by side and face to face with real people. For many older players who have limited workplace and family connections, it's our primary social outlet. It's hard to put a value on this vibrant "person to person" dynamic. Mix in the rush of mood-boosting endorphins that exercise provides and it's little wonder why we become addicted to our happy little game.

Pickleball is also finding its way into the public consciousness. You can now catch matches on TV, YouTube, and other forums. It's inspiring to watch top pros do their thing, and it's fun to see our sport popping up in strange places. There was even a recent video of Chicago Cubs pitchers playing pickleball on a makeshift court in the bullpen at a baseball game. Maybe someday pickleball will qualify as an Olympic sport. . . who knows? It's exciting to be in on the initial stages of this boom. And you can say that you were there when it happened!

⊙ Pickleball Events, Venues, and Tourism

As the sport explodes in popularity, so do the variety of opportunities to enjoy the game. You can participate in tournaments at your ranking level or watch the pros do their thing. Every week of the year features local, regional, or national tournaments, and if you can't be there in person, Pickleball Channel online provides live streaming and archived tournament footage that you can find on YouTube. At USApickleball.org and globalpickleball.network, you can find information on tournaments, court locations, and much more. Go to www.playtimescheduler.com to create and join play sessions with other players in your area, or go to www.places2play.org to find (duh...) places to play near you.

Neighborhood courts or local clubs are where most of us get our pickleball fix. But new pickleball venues are taking things to another level. "Chicken N Pickle" in Kansas City is one of the original multiuse facilities, featuring food, drink, and entertainment options.

Many other venues have imitated and expanded this concept at indoor and outdoor locations. New complexes with multiple courts are being built throughout the country. As the demand for pickleball skyrockets, communities and entrepreneurs are rushing to supply venues that offer quality and entertainment, making the pickleball experience better than ever for us devotees.

Your author, enjoying the good life in Mexico with friends.

Pickleball clubs regularly schedule group lessons to introduce new players to the game or help their current players develop new skills. Many clubs also offer multi-day clinics featuring top pros and coaches. If you have plans to travel to Florida, California, or other pickleball hotspots, why not contact clubs in the area and combine "pickleball business" with pleasure?

Pickleball is also the magnet that has spawned a new business model that caters to the more adventurous senior player: "destination pickleball travel". I have included some examples in Appendix 1 that offer options to play, explore, and receive quality instruction domestically or at exotic locales. Some companies specialize in pickleball "boot camps" with intensive instruction, while others seek more of a balance between pickleball and tourism. Determine what *your* priorities are before signing up for a trip.*

Even some cruise ships are getting in on the action, anticipating the desire of their older, active customers to play and socialize at sea. Hotels and resorts are catching on as well. If you love to travel and love to play, what could be better?

Pickleball addiction is one of the healthiest "disorders" you could have. It feeds the need for the senior athlete who wants to stay active and engaged with their world. And the options to satisfy our craving will only continue to expand whether we seek to play, watch, improve our skills, or travel.

---

* Go to www.mikebranon.com/travel to see a couple of travel articles on my website that go into more detail on specific locations in Mexico and Costa Rica.

PLAYING BETTER

So, we've established that pickleball is a popular, addictive game that's great for seniors. I know what many of you are probably thinking, "That's great, Mike. Now how can I ramp up my game and beat that obnoxious couple who always wins and celebrates a little *too* much?"

Of course, when it comes to instruction, one size doesn't fit all. For example, a third shot drive may work for a stronger player, but if you can't generate enough power and make too many errors with your drive, a third shot drop is usually your best bet. Even then, your decision depends on your opponents' position on the court, their ability to handle power versus finesse, and other factors as well.

Another pitfall of "one size fits all" instruction is that everyone has a different skill set and physical capabilities. I may insist that you rush to the kitchen line after every return of serve, but if you physically can't move quickly enough, there are other strategies you can use (more on that later).

The subject matter for most of this book applies to all of us, but the instruction I provide in the following pages is geared toward the majority of senior players from beginners up to a 4.0 rating, who aspire to improve the quality of their game. If you're an advanced player, use what you can and skip over what you have already mastered. If you're just starting out, some of the instruction in this section will seem like it's written in a foreign language, but hang in there! As you learn the game, most of this stuff will begin to make sense. And I hope this book serves as a continuing resource as you learn and improve over the years.*

Beware of online instruction or books (like this one!) that provide information without on-court feedback. You may think you're doing what is recommended but might be missing something you can't feel or see such as proper footwork, paddle position, or body mechanics. You can undoubtedly improve your game by studying videos online or reading good books. Just remember that live feedback from a trusted coach or advanced player ensures that you are properly integrating new skills.

---

* If you are new to the game, I have included some basic definitions, court dimensions, and rules in Appendix 2 to give you a head start. Feel free to go there before diving into this chapter.

I may not be able to give you live feedback in this book, but for you visual learners, I will provide you with links to videos that complement my written instruction. Take videos of your games and drills as well—it can be eye-opening. A picture (or a video) can be worth a thousand words. The combination of written and video instruction will enhance your understanding and enable you to integrate these essential skills.

Many players spend a lot of time and money on instruction but neglect an essential step in the process—they don't write down or record new information. I don't know about you, but this old guy is just happy when he remembers to bring his tennis shoes to the court. The best way to commit anything to memory is to write it down and review it regularly. I keep a pickleball journal that includes almost every nugget that I've picked up along the way. You don't need to be as obsessive as me, but having a resource that you can refer to with key concepts keeps you focused on the basics that enable you to bring your best game to the court every day.

I often ask my students to tell me one or two things they learned and have been working on from the previous lesson. If they can't give me an immediate answer, I know that they are not getting the full benefit of my instruction by writing down key points. I also may take a few minutes at the end of a lesson to do a quick video review so that my students can refer to it when they want. Again, integrating what you have learned requires repetition and review. Do what works for you.

The main concept I teach is the **KISS** system. **K**eep **I**t **S**imple (the final **"S"** can stand for Sweetheart, Stupid, or Superstar. Your choice...). Proper footwork and paddle position are the simple keys to consistent play. Once you get to the ball and are in the right hitting position, it's just a matter of executing the shot you have made thousands of times. If you set up properly to hit consistent shots, you will hit more consistent shots. It doesn't get any simpler than that.

My advice is suitable for players of all ages, but I will give specific tips for senior players when appropriate. Many of us seniors don't need to make many concessions to age—we can still give the younger generation more than they can handle. However, some of us could use a few strategies to compensate for a lack of power or mobility. Again, pickleball isn't brain surgery—simple concepts and fundamentals enable you to play with less errors, and winning pickleball is all about reducing errors and playing the percentages.

⊛ Starting Out the Right Way

Group or individual lessons go a long way toward making pickleball as rewarding as possible. If you're going to do this right, why not instill proper fundamentals from the beginning rather than needing to unlearn your initial random whacking at the ball. This can be especially true of tennis players who must adjust their mechanics to succeed at pickleball. Find a coach or other resource that resonates with you and start out on the right foot. If you've been playing for a while, it's never too late to reboot your game if you're not getting the results you want. Doing anything well maximizes enjoyment and motivates you to excel even more. The game is *so* much more rewarding when it's played correctly. Otherwise, it's like doing a crossword puzzle with no clues—you can fill in the letters, but it doesn't make much sense. Get the information that gives you the best opportunity to solve the pickleball puzzle.

You can find these lessons quite easily in most areas, and online information is readily available as well. I've listed links to some of my favorite resources in Appendix 1 at the end of this book.

⊛ How Do I Get More Out of My Pickleball Experience?

Two words: keep learning. I love watching my older students light up when they learn a new technique. Their inner child rejoices at the spark of discovery, and they can't wait to catch their unsuspecting opponents off guard with their new skills. Above all, keep this in mind:

Pickleball is easy to learn and hard to master.

I look at this as another "Pickleball Positive". You can

simply enjoy hitting the ball around with your friends without any designs on becoming an advanced player. If that's what you want, knock yourself out (not literally... try to stay upright and avoid hard objects like poles and other people's paddles). However, if you want to take your game to the next level, you must continue to practice and learn. As time goes on, new equipment, new techniques, and new shots evolve, so we must evolve as well. Even top pros share that they keep learning too. Pickleball school is never out of session.

If you are motivated to improve and thrive, pickleball is a challenge that you never completely solve, but love every minute of. Shot selection is of supreme importance. You may be skilled at hitting a particular shot but must have the patience to wait for the right moment to use it. Even the best players are always seeking new ways to befuddle, surprise, and discombobulate their opponents. It's a rush to figure out a new shot, spring it on your pals, and watch the amazement on their faces as the ball shoots past them or off them.

If you feel that you aren't consistently playing as well as you would like, you must either put in the work to improve your game or accept where you're at and find games commensurate with your ability. If you're not as good as you wish you were, join the club! There is always someone better at everything in life!* *Just remember to keep putting yourself in*

---

* Okay. There is that one person who is better than everyone, but who needs the pressure of being #1? I kinda like being #48,923—that way, if I have a bad game and drop a few hundred spots in the cosmic rankings, nobody notices.

a position to have fun—playing at the level and with the people that make you happy to be on the court.

It's important to understand the process of learning and improving. Otherwise, you might become frustrated with your progress and abandon ship before you even set sail. There are four stages we go through when we learn any new skill:

Stage 1: Unconscious Incompetence

In this stage, you are like a child. You don't know how to do anything. You don't even know how much you don't know. This is the moment you first saw people playing pickleball and said to yourself, "Huh?".

Stage 2: Conscious Incompetence

You are painfully aware that you don't know what you're doing. This is like feeling clueless on your first date or missing the ball completely and thinking that maybe a lesson or two would be a good idea.

Stage 3: Conscious Competence

You took those lessons and have played quite a bit. You know what to do but it's so darn hard to do it because you keep having to think about what you're *supposed* to do and end up playing mechanically and indecisively: "*So many shot options in my head–which one do I choose?*"

Stage 4: Unconscious Competence

This is where your game blossoms as your skills become second nature. This is the "flow state"—action and awareness become one, and achievement becomes effortless. On the court, you automatically end up in the right position and seem to have the ball on a string. The game slows down for you. You feel like you have plenty of time to hit the proper shot. You still make errors, of course, but they are fewer and far between.

Unfortunately, we all must go through the first three stages to arrive at our destination. The goal is to spend less time in each stage along the way, reducing the suffering and increasing the joy of learning and playing. We can get stuck in certain stages. That's not an indictment of who we are; it's just that few endeavors in life are mastered. Wherever you are or wherever you end up with your pickleball game, it's essential to be aware of these stages and be kind to yourself. Self-compassion is the antidote to self-judgment.*

---

* I write at length in my first book, *Pickleball & The Art of Living*, about the benefits of hardwiring happiness into our brains. Unfortunately, we are evolutionarily wired to dwell on the negative and gloss over the positive. Next time you play, do yourself a favor and shrug off your poor shots without making any negative physical or verbal reaction—and spend an extra couple of seconds after a good shot to pat yourself on the back and appreciate your fabulous talent and good looks. Just make sure to keep it limited to a couple of seconds and avoid any excessive fist-pumping or moonwalking.

The keys to reaching unconscious competence are open to debate. There are many opinions about the best way to play, but I believe that the twin pillars of pickleball proficiency are "Physical" and "Mental". For many senior players, the physical game can face limitations, but we can use strategy and a positive attitude to enjoy pickleball as much or more than players half our age. However, there is no denying that pickleball is a physical game. Let's examine how we can make this part of our game the best it can be.

⦿ The Physical Game

When building anything, you need to start with the right tools. You can have the best design and blueprints, but it takes a skilled craftsman with the right tools to make a project come to life. In pickleball, you build your game with the actual shots. This is your foundation.

Knowing when to use each shot is the strategic part of the game. I will discuss strategy in the following section, but for now, let's master the shots that enable you to execute your strategy effectively.

If you are a more advanced player, please bear with me as I go into detail about skills you already have in your arsenal. You may still find some concepts that merit renewed focus—not just physical skills, but more nuanced topics such as strategy, intention, patience, and mindset. Maybe this instruction will also enable you to better help others who look to you for support and advice. If you're a fit, powerful player, disregard the concessions to age that I will occasionally address. Just run your fingers through your beautiful, full head of hair and be grateful for your winning smile and prodigious forehand.

Senior pickleballers are a diverse group and I want to make sure that the needs of the less experienced and more "life experienced" players are addressed. Remember, no matter where you are on the spectrum of senior players, it never hurts to reinforce the fundamentals that enable you to play winning pickleball.

⊙ The Shots

You must develop the proper technique for every shot, whether it's a dink, volley, serve, return, groundstroke, drop shot, overhead, or lob. These are the basic tools that build your game. Every good shot requires the proper combination of paddle position, footwork, direction, and pace. Incorporate each element to promote consistency and accuracy.

Use a continental grip for all your shots. Simply hold the paddle in front of you, perpendicular to the ground, and shake hands with it. This grip is versatile in that it allows you to hit every shot without needing to change your grip when the ball comes at you quickly.

Paddle position is vital. In general, keep your paddle in front of you at contact and follow through directly to your target. Also, try to stay as compact as possible—when you reach to the side for the ball or play it from behind your body, you don't see the ball as well. This is especially true with dinks and volleys. Many errors I see my students make are a variation on contacting the ball too far away from the optimal contact zone. Where exactly is this zone?

If you hold your arms out in front of you at 45-degree angles from your body, you are defining the optimal contact zone for almost all your shots within that 90-degree bear-hug range. When you make contact off to the side or behind your hips, you don't see the ball as well, you lose sight of your opponents' position on the court, and you are forced to use your little muscles in your wrists and forearms to manipulate the ball weakly over the net. Instead, stay compact, elbows close to the body, and play the ball in front of you as much as possible. I will soon give you tips on how to use footwork to stay behind the ball, increasing your consistency and accuracy.

A square paddle face to your target *at impact and through impact* is essential. Remember that being able to put the ball where you want to on the court is more important than power. That's how the founders intended pickleball to be played so that people of all ages and physical abilities could enjoy the game!

Keep in mind that every shot I describe is designed to get you to increase your skill at the Non-Volley Zone (NVZ)* or kitchen, as it is usually called. *Pickleball is won at the kitchen line* and lost with every step you are behind the kitchen line. It's a positional tug-of-war, except you're trying to push your opponents away from the line and pull yourself up to it.

Pickleball is like real estate. It's all about location, location, location. When you take up prime real estate at the kitchen line, contact the ball in that upscale neighborhood in front of your body, and learn to place the ball in proper locations, your pickleball game will appreciate like a beachfront mansion.

"Push" Shots and "Hit" Shots

There are two types of shots in pickleball, and they require different body mechanics and paddle angles. A "push" shot is a dink, third shot drop, reset, or any ball you contact that is intended to bounce low in the kitchen. It requires touch and accuracy. A "hit" shot is any other shot that seeks to drive

---

* If you are new to the game, refer to Appendix 2 for details on the rules of pickleball and the location of the Non-Volley Zone (aka kitchen). SPOILER ALERT! It's a zone where you can't volley.

the ball with some degree of power. Let's examine the "push" shots first.

Most people who take up pickleball are more comfortable with hitting at the ball—"See ball. Hit ball" is a natural reaction. "Push" shots require overcoming this instinct in favor of placing the ball low and softly at your opponents' feet. As you make this shot, visualize the "big muscles" doing all the work. In other words, you are pushing with your legs and core to some degree, and to a greater degree, *you are pushing from the shoulder.* This makes for a more consistent, repeatable stroke. *Do not* use the little muscles in the hands, wrists, and forearm to try to manipulate the ball to your target. This will cause tension and inconsistent results. (If this seems confusing, watch the linked videos to clarify this technique.)

When executing these shots, the paddle face must be open or facing upward to some degree to create loft. The feeling is one of smoothly pushing the ball up with almost no backswing and dropping it over the net. When you are deep in the court, these drop shots enable you to move forward and play from the kitchen line. When you are playing balls hit at your feet, pushing the ball is common sense from a physics perspective—if you hit a low ball hard, it is usually destined for the net or out of play. Learning these shots and implementing them at the proper time will make your game the best it can be. Otherwise, you will be reduced to hitting and hoping, making low percentage shots without any kind of a game plan.

One of the great things about pickleball is that "push" shots level the playing field for older players. We must take advantage of this feature, using placement and touch to establish optimal forward position and keep the ball low and un-attackable. When we play from forward in the court, mobility matters less than ability.

◔ The Dink

Dinking is a concept that is unique to pickleball among racquet/paddle sports. It can be the great equalizer when playing with bangers, limiting their ability to hit aggressively at your team. If they try to hit the ball hard from the kitchen area, they will usually hit it into the net or long. It requires patience to dink well. Often, the first person to flinch and try to win the point with an ill-advised hard shot will lose.

When you watch the pros, it seems like they never miss, sometimes hitting 50 or more dinks in a row before someone attacks. What is the secret to their skill? Well, first of all, they're pros. They've hit hundreds of thousands of dinks. But if you watch them carefully, you'll see that they do three common things that you can emulate.

First, they get *low*. They bend at the knees, not at the waist, so they are balanced over their feet with a low center of gravity. To hit up on the ball, you must get your paddle below the ball.

Second, they *set* the paddle face early to an open position that dictates the arc of the ball. And they keep that paddle face at the same angle and square to their target through impact and on the follow-through.

Third, they *push* from their core and shoulder with a

relaxed arm as they contact the ball. Pushing with a tight grip or using the little muscles in the hand, wrist, and forearm to manipulate the paddle creates tension and inconsistency.

As I teach my beginner students to dink, I say, *"Low. Set. Push."* "Low" encourages the bending of the knees and positioning the paddle low to the ground, while "Set" is the prompt to place the paddle in the optimal position/angle as soon as possible. I say the word "Push" softly to encourage a smooth, flowing stroke from the shoulder. Even if you're a more advanced player, try experimenting with this technique and see if you notice an improvement in your consistency. Here's your first video that shows how to dink consistently and effectively:

Video #1: DINKING ESSENTIALS: LOW, SET, PUSH.
Watch this video now at https://www.mikebranon.com/joy

Another must for dinking and the other "push" shots is to use little or no backswing. Meet the ball out in front of you and extend your paddle squarely toward your target to maximize consistency.

As you dink, you don't want to feed the ball directly to your opponent on a nice high hop where they can easily handle it (especially not to their forehand). Move them around with angled shots to get them out of position or go down the middle to create confusion. Even though this is a soft shot, it can still be an aggressive one. I often target the left foot of my right-handed opponent at the net, causing them to back up or be indecisive about taking the ball out of the air on their backhand.

Finally, as you compete against better players, the cross-court dink is usually the smart play. It gives you more room for error and is not as easy to attack as the ball hit straight across to them. There is much more to say about dinking, but if you follow these basic strategies and techniques, you will find that your dink game can level the playing field against more powerful or younger players.

⊙ The Third Shot Drop

Ah, the third shot drop... Much has been written about this shot and rightfully so. *In fact, a dependable third shot drop may be the most vital stroke to master if you want to take your game to the next level.*

After the return of serve, the intelligent returner will hustle to the kitchen line after hitting the ball deep in the court. The serving team must let the ball bounce and often find themselves deep in the court, facing a wall of players at the kitchen line (okay, only two players, but sometimes it seems like a wall). What to do?

Beginning players are usually just happy to get the ball over the net on the third shot, but of course, those shots often float high and are easily put away by the other team. If you have a powerful, *consistent* groundstroke, you can hit a "third shot drive", hopefully handcuffing your opponent, creating an

THE JOY OF PICKLEBALL

error or a weak short shot that you can come in on and either drive or dink as the situation demands.

However, for many of us, especially if we can't hit the ball powerfully and accurately, the percentage play is to hit a soft arcing ball low over the net so that it can't be attacked, enabling us to move forward toward the kitchen line. Until we join the other team at the kitchen, we are at a decided disadvantage. This ain't tennis! Banging from the baseline when the opponents have control of the net is a trusty recipe for losing at pickleball.

The problem is that making this shot is counterintuitive to the beginner or intermediate player—"You mean you want me to hit a soft, floating ball when I'm all the way back here?" Every coach has heard a variation on that comment. However, this is the best strategy to overcome the disadvantage of being the serving team. So, how do you hit this tricky shot?

The keys to making a solid, dependable third shot drop are set-up, body mechanics, and remembering that it is a "push" shot. If you take a big backswing and *hit* this shot, you will need to decelerate your stroke as you make contact. Deceleration is the kiss of death in any sport.

Almost every shot you make in pickleball involves accelerating the paddle through contact with a follow-through that is longer than the backswing with the paddle face square to the target at impact.

A short or negligible backswing is especially important to executing a proper third shot drop. You generate enough power to clear the net with proper body mechanics and a long follow-through. In fact, I recommend thinking of a third shot drop as simply a dink with a longer follow-through. *Bonus tip: on the forehand drop shot, a secret to eliminating a long backswing is to keep your paddle in front of your right knee (for a right-hander) so it can't swing back behind you.*

It's also essential to get your legs involved by stepping into the ball from a low position. This adds effortless power to the stroke and gets you moving forward toward the kitchen line, which is your destination after making the shot. Again, "Low, Set, Push" is an effective way to feel this shot.

A crucial key to a dependable third shot drop is to get in the proper position to do all of the above. Move your feet quickly as the return of serve approaches, then once you're in the perfect position, it's just a matter of executing the same shot over and over. If you don't move quickly into position, you make a difficult shot almost impossible by having to lunge or backpedal as the ball arrives. *Be quick to the ball, but don't hurry the stroke.*

Video #2: MASTERING THE THIRD SHOT DROP
Watch this video now at https://www.mikebranon.com/joy

Now you know how to execute this shot; where should you hit it? If the returner doesn't make it all the way to the kitchen line, you want to drop or hit the ball at their feet as they come in. If the returner gets to the kitchen quickly, I prefer to hit the vast majority of third shot drops to the backhand corner of the player on the right (or ad, for you tennis players) side of the court as you face them. Most right-handed players can't aggressively attack balls hit low to their backhand. I'll go down the middle occasionally, but I try to avoid setting up a potentially aggressive forehand. The advantage of hitting this shot consistently to one or two spots is that you groove your stroke and reduce indecision. Remember, keep it simple. Above all, do what works for you.

Great! Now you know how and where to hit (push) the ball, what next? Well, you can stand there and admire your third shot drop as it floats beautifully into the kitchen. The problem is that your opponent will probably hit it back deep to you. Then you must hit a fifth shot drop and then a seventh shot drop—you get the idea. After hitting a good drop, you must follow it up to the kitchen. If possible, hightail it all the way up to the kitchen line. You should follow the path of the ball as you move forward as this puts you in the optimal position for the next shot. If you can't get all the way in, pause as your opponent is about to hit and be prepared to hit a much easier drop over the net before making it to the kitchen line.

Finally, when do you *not* hit a third shot drop? When the service return is short and bounces high enough, go into driving mode and pound the ball between or at your opponents. And if the returner doesn't get to the kitchen line as you're ready to hit the third shot, drive it deep at their feet to force a weak shot and follow that drive to the kitchen.

If you don't develop an effective third shot drop, your progress will plateau. It is especially suited to the senior player who may need to rely on finesse and guile to play their best. When you develop and hone this skill, your game will take a big step forward and you will be on the path to become the best player you can be.

⊙ The Reset

When you're back in the court and a ball is hit hard at your feet, your chances of hitting the ball hard and keeping it in play are minimal. You're much better off holding your position, getting as low as possible, softening your grip, and blocking or short-hopping the ball with an open paddle face. The open face takes the pace off the ball and allows it to arc into the kitchen. When a hard-hit ball handcuffs you on a volley at the net, softly blocking the ball into the kitchen may be your best bet.

In either case, you are basically resetting the point by putting the ball back soft and low over the net and landing it in the kitchen if possible. This short-circuits your opponents' attempts to overpower you because you are forcing them to hit up on the ball from low and close to the net. Admittedly, this is the most difficult "push" shot to execute. At this point, you're simply trying to make the best of a bad situation. So, don't be too hard on yourself when you can't pull this shot off... at least you're giving yourself a chance to get back in the point.

When resetting a ball hit hard at your body, you must again open the paddle face, but only slightly—you want to feel like you're catching the ball and taking the pace off it so that it drops softly over the net. *This is a great shot to practice in drills.* Once you hit enough of them, your touch will improve and you will feel the satisfaction of digging yourself out of a bad situation and saving points from the dead. It can really turn the momentum of a match.

Video #3: THE RESET: STOP, DROP, AND GET BACK ON A ROLL
Watch this video now at https://www.mikebranon.com/joy

If you played tennis, racquetball, or table tennis, you must adjust your mentality and develop the skills necessary to master the finesse aspect of pickleball. The good news is that racket sports experience gives you a head start on mastering the "hit" shots. These are the shots that were not mentioned above, such as serves, groundstrokes, volleys, and overheads. Let's explore some features of these shots now.

⊙ The Serve

Serving can be a weapon in pickleball, but except for some talented players, it is mainly a way to get the point started. The main requirement is to get the ball in play. There's nothing more frustrating in pickleball than hitting your serve out. Accuracy should be your primary goal, followed by depth and location. Whether you bounce the ball or drop it directly to your paddle, follow through to your target with a square paddle face through impact. Accelerate through the ball and use a shorter backswing to promote consistent contact. A senior player who might be lacking strength can benefit from stepping into the shot, extending your follow-through on a low to high path, and cocking your wrist to add power.

⊚ Groundstrokes

The forehand is usually the weapon of choice to overpower your opponents. Some folks have a potent backhand as well, but most of us use our forehand to either apply pressure from deep in the court or hit winners from up close. Whether you approach the ball from the side with shoulders turned or face the ball and use more of a "wristy" stroke from in front of the hip, the idea is to keep the ball low. High shots will fly out or set up for easy volleys from the other team.

The backhand groundstroke is usually not a powerful weapon for most players unless they have brought a wicked two-handed stroke with them from tennis. You can make up for a less powerful backhand by focusing on keeping it low over the net. Making solid contact with the backhand, whether you hit a topspin, flat, or slice stroke, requires that you turn your lead shoulder and hit through the ball with a long follow-through. Failure to turn your body results in a weak, slapping motion with a bent arm at contact.

The best way to keep the ball low on your groundstrokes is to start your backswing with the paddle low (around knee level) and swing up and through the ball to a high finish around the shoulder. Make sure to make contact in front of you. When combined with a flat to slightly closed paddle face through contact, topspin is created, powering the ball forward and downward as it clears the net. (If this seems confusing for you novice players, watch the link to the video in this section to get a clearer picture.)

Another key element is early preparation. As soon as you see the ball heading toward you, turn and present the paddle into the contact position as you move to the anticipated contact point. This is much more effective than running to the ball with your paddle at your side, then taking a rushed backswing and stroke once you arrive. Take long strides to reach this contact point as soon as possible, then take a series of short steps to put yourself in the perfect position. This early preparation enables you to hit from the same position every time without having to rush and flail at the ball. You will be in balance, make a consistent, relaxed swing, and reduce errors.

It's important not to fall in love with your forehand from deep in the court when your opponents are at the kitchen line. Skilled players at the kitchen line can easily dismantle most baseliners in pickleball. When you hit any groundstroke, don't assume you've hit a winner—be ready to move forward and take advantage of a solid shot. Again, the kitchen line is usually where you win the game.

There is too much to say about the possible variations on the groundstrokes here. Suffice to say that footwork and early preparation put you in the optimal position and proper body mechanics such as turning and using a short-to-long, low-to-high stroke will go a long way toward making your shots consistent and effective. One other essential factor is staying low and level throughout the stroke. Many players miss when they rise up or open their "non-hitting" shoulder (on the forehand) as they make contact. This is often the result of over-hitting. Trust your stroke by staying down and compact through contact. This will keep the ball low and reduce errors.

Video #4: GROUNDSTROKES: POWER AND CONSISTENCY
Watch this video now at https://www.mikebranon.com/joy

⦿ Volleys

Volleys are one of the most fun strokes in pickleball. Most of us love the quick back and forth up at the net as we try to outduel our opponents from close range. The most important part of volleying is keeping the paddle in front of you. It should be about a foot in front of your chest so your slightly bent arm can extend through contact and create power. This enables you to play the ball instead of the ball playing you. It also takes away reaction time from the other team. *Ideally, your paddle should always be making contact in front of the kitchen line as you volley.*

If you are volleying when the other team is back in the

court, the smart play is usually to keep them back with deep volleys. Alternatively, you can angle the ball off the court or drop it softly into the kitchen. You don't want to hit short, high volleys that they can get to and follow into the net.

When you volley with all players at the kitchen line, keep the ball low. If you get a ball that is high enough, be aggressive and hit down at the feet, down the middle, or at an angle. Avoid hitting balls directly at your opponents' paddles. Sometimes when we practice, we get in the habit of feeding each other on volleys. Instead, if you're hitting at the other player, it's effective to target the right armpit of a right-hander as this can handcuff them as they try to flip the paddle from backhand to forehand.

For older players who don't have the snap on the volleys that they want, remember that location is your best weapon. Keeping the ball low and hitting it where your opponent must lunge for it can make up for a lack of power. Avoid opening the paddle face and slicing under your volleys if the ball is above the net; this results in pop-ups and poor contact. Instead, drive the ball aggressively with a flat or slightly closed face for a more powerful stroke. Pretend like you're swatting a fly—don't stop your paddle at contact. Follow through!

Stay low and keep your lower body active as you volley. When you have time to slide in front of a ball that is to the side, you put yourself in a more powerful position behind the ball instead of reaching for it. When you reach to the side without shifting your body, you lose power and jab at the ball with a weaker, "wristy" stroke. Instead, imagine a boxer throwing a short, compact right cross as you hit a forehand volley—the power comes from striking directly from in front of the shoulder area, not from way off to the side or behind your body. On your backhand volley, try to hit the ball from in front of your chest by moving to the ball. This movement enables you to "punch" the ball from that optimal 90-degree area in front of your body that I mentioned previously. Again, keep your paddle in front, body low and balanced, up on the balls of your feet, and ready for battle!

Video #5: THE VOLLEY: KEYS TO DOMINANCE AT THE NET
Watch this video now at https://www.mikebranon.com/joy

◌ Lobs

Lobs are best used sparingly but they can be very effective, especially among older players. Many of us find it much easier to hit a lob than to track one down. It can be frustrating to play against a skillful lob artist when you do everything right, get position at the kitchen line, then look up helplessly as the ball floats over your head. So, how do you hit a lob and defend against one?

The best time to lob is when you and the other team are at the kitchen line. Lobs should be disguised as dinks until the last moment when you lift the ball deep in the court, preferably over the backhand shoulder of either opponent. You can even lob off a volley to add an extra element of surprise. Lobbing from the back of the court is much more difficult to pull off as the other team has more time to move back and hit an overhead.

To defend a lob, it's important to communicate. It's usually preferable for the player who has *not* been lobbed over to track the lob diagonally so that they have a better angle to the ball. You NEVER want to backpedal more than a step or two to hit an overhead on a lob. For older players in particular, this is like going for a walk in traffic. I have seen broken wrists and concussions result from backpedaling, tripping, and falling backward. Instead, turn your body and track the high ball like an outfielder in baseball, running back on an angle while tracking the ball over one shoulder. If a 25-year-old top athlete doesn't backpedal to get a ball, why would you?

If you can hit a lob out of the air with an overhead, that is obviously the best play. However, if you can't get to the ball in the air, try to get to the side of the ball as it bounces and execute a soft drop back over the net. Sometimes the only thing you can do is lunge and lob the ball back as high and deep as you can, giving your team time to take up a solid defensive position for the next shot.

When your partner scrambles to return a lob, where should *you* go? I advise retreating to a position on the opposite side of the court about 10 feet inside the baseline. If your partner can drop the ball into the kitchen, you have time to move up in the court. If the ball is lobbed back to the other team, you have time to move back and take up a defensive position with your partner.

Video #6: ALL YOU NEED IS LOB
Watch this video now at https://www.mikebranon.com/joy

⚙ The Overhead

You do all the work to get to the kitchen line, deftly mixing drops and dinks. Looking good! Finally, you force your opponent to hit a high, juicy ball that you can crush, and... "ARGHHH!!!". You botch the put-away.

It's extremely frustrating to miss those easy shots. How do you make your overhead a consistent, potent weapon? *The key is making a more compact stroke, especially at the kitchen line.* Some players develop a habit where they bring the paddle way back, almost scratching their back with the paddle as they prepare to hit. By the time the paddle returns to hitting position, it might be facing anywhere but square to the target, resulting in a variety of wayward shots. Instead, shorten the backswing and snap through as you strike the ball, feeling the wrist do the work. You can still turn your shoulders and rotate your lower body to generate power, just shorten the stroke.

Also, avoid "jack-knifing". Keep your chest up and aim for a spot around 10' inside the baseline. Unlike a tennis ball, which will compress and bounce high and out of play, a pickleball will actually sit up when you hit down hard on it and make for a relatively easy return when your opponents are deep in the court.

Finally, learn to execute the "VolleyPop". On a ball that is hit from just above your head, down to around chest level at the net, you can squat down with your paddle vertical and in front of you and pop the ball down the middle with a short, wristy stroke. (It feels like swatting a fly or hammering a nail—and you wouldn't take a big backswing to hammer a nail unless you don't mind crooked nails and smashed fingers). It's more effective and powerful than hitting a standard volley because it's actually a quasi-overhead. Keep the paddle face square to your target through impact to avoid slicing across the ball and losing accuracy. When the other team is back, this short stroke also makes it easier to angle the ball off the court. For older or less powerful players, this technique may be more effective at ending the point.

⊛ Specialty Shots

There are other shots you can play at the kitchen line that require a decent skill level such as flicks, rollovers, ATPs, and Ernes. I won't cover all of these in detail here, but feel free to look them up online and play around with them. I have included a short video on a couple of these shots later in this chapter to get you started.

Now that we have examined the shots, what are the

common elements that make every shot better? *The problem is often not the shot itself... it's what happens before the shot is even hit.*

◌ Footwork and Positioning

No matter what type of shot you hit, footwork and positioning are crucial to proper execution. Many players tell me that their dink, drop, or backhand needs help. Invariably, the problem is their set-up—they aren't getting low and setting the paddle face on their "push" shots or they fail to prepare early and turn their body on their "hit" shots as needed. When you play with proper positioning and body mechanics, your shots become simpler and more reliable. If you freeze-frame a top tennis or pickleball player just as they are about to strike the ball, you will see that they are in perfect balance and have a consistent impact point most of the time. Every picture of them at contact looks identical. Your goal should also be to put yourself in the same optimal position to succeed every time.

You must be on the balls of your feet, ready to make quick steps so that you are in the ideal position as often as possible, with your weight balanced or slightly forward. When you don't move properly, you end up leaning, reaching, lunging, or falling backward. There are times when you must do all of the above out of necessity when your opponent makes a great shot, but more often than not, you have time to move quickly to put yourself in the optimal position.

Dedicate yourself to moving your feet. On a dink, a quick

shuffle step can mean the difference between a controlled shot and a lunging, off-balance pop-up. On a third shot drop or groundstroke, a quick step back on a hard shot can put you in position to plant your back foot and push or hit the shot to your target, also allowing you to move forward more easily and quickly to the kitchen. On a volley, you can use a slide step (one quick step to the side as the other foot slides with you) to get your body behind the ball, putting you in a more powerful position to consistently strike the ball rather than reaching.

All this footwork relies on being up on the balls of your feet with your paddle in ready position. As we get older, we tend to lose that bounce in our step. However, when you're on the court, dedicate yourself to play up on the balls of your feet as best as you can. It allows you to react quickly and get in the proper position to hit better shots. Try not to play like Frankenstein's monster with a hangover—flatfooted and slow to react. You should feel nimble, balanced, and ready to move in any direction. *As you move into position on all of these shots, be careful not to get "happy feet", move too much, and find yourself out of position for the next shot.*

Positioning also involves your location on the court. You must move to the kitchen line at every opportunity to take control of points. *The kitchen line is where the game is won* (have I mentioned that before?).

One of the most important positioning tips for novice players involves the serve and return. When you serve, stay at the baseline as you await the return. If you wander into the court, you won't be able to handle a return hit at your feet.

Even if you get the ball over the net, you'll be moving backward at contact and unable to hit an effective third shot.

When you return serve, start far enough back (depending on the power of your opponent's serve) so that you have a forward weight shift as you hit the ball and can move quickly to the kitchen line. Failure to do either of these two basic things is just giving points away.

Repeat after me:
Serve: Stay
Return: Run

As you run in after your return, you may not get all the way to the kitchen line as your opponent is ready to hit the next shot. (TIP: If you're not as fast as you used to be, an effective way to give yourself more time to reach the kitchen line is to hit a deep, looping return.) If you can't make it all the way in, *stop and get in ready position* as your opponent is about to play the ball. You want to run in, *but you don't want to be running as you hit or as your opponent is hitting*. This makes it almost impossible to control your shot.

The techniques above require no skill—they simply put you in *position* to hit the best shots possible and win more points.

Video #7: FOOTWORK AND PREPARATION:
THE KEYS TO GREAT SHOT-MAKING
Watch this video now at https://www.mikebranon.com/joy

Many players will focus on their missed shots without realizing that these misses are often a direct consequence of improper body position as they contact the ball or suboptimal location on the court before the ball is struck by their opponent. Your shots will magically improve when you are in the right position every time.

⊙ Preparation

Preparation goes hand in hand with positioning. Not only does preparation involve proper pre-shot positioning on the court and being up on the balls of your feet, but it also depends on posture and paddle position. It's hard to play effective pickleball when you look like you're standing in line at the grocery store, standing

upright with one hand hanging by your side, maybe even look-ing at your cell phone. You might as well be wearing a t-shirt that says, "Hit Me!". Keeping both hands up keeps your body square and balanced and discourages you from letting your paddle drop. When you're at the kitchen, always have your hands and paddle up, expecting a hard shot.

The good news is that when you are properly prepared to hit a shot, you're getting a great glute and leg workout while you wait (and you thought you were just having fun...). You should keep your knees slightly bent, up on the balls of your feet, stance somewhat wide, butt somewhat low, chin up, and weight balanced evenly, ready to move in any direction. *If you set up like an athlete, you play like an athlete.*

There are varying opinions about the "ready" paddle posi-tion when at the kitchen line. I prefer keeping the bottom edge of the paddle slightly above the navel at about 10:30-11:00 for a right-hander (if the paddle pointing straight at your opponent is 12:00) favoring the backhand. I find this position especially helpful when a shot may come back at me quickly. From this position, I can square the paddle and reset or attack even if I must "chicken-wing" a ball hit a bit to my forehand side. This works great for me and most of my students—but as the kids say these days, "You do you!"

As your opponent is ready to strike the ball, you should stop your forward motion and assume your ready position. Again, running through the ball as you make contact or as the ball is hit at you makes it difficult to control your shot. If you are back in the court and expect a hard shot, squat low with your paddle low as well. This gives you more of an opportunity to block the ball back when your opponent wisely hits at your feet.

Another aspect of preparation is moving into optimal hitting position as soon as you begin to pick up clues as to your opponents' intentions. These clues can come in the form of a longer backswing, telltale stance, or paddle face angle. Crafty senior players pick up on these clues and get a head start on preparing their feet and paddle position to execute the best shot available. Beginners will sometimes wait until the ball is almost to them and then take a hurried backswing and hit at the ball without much rhythm or intention. It's amazing how much "quicker" you are when your observation and anticipation give you a head start to get to balls sooner and in a better position.

I love legendary basketball coach, John Wooden's advice: *"Be quick, but don't hurry"*. Move quickly into position, then relax and let the stroke flow. No matter what type of shot you hit, this technique will result in the best pickleball you can play.

Defense

Defense is an underrated skill. Again, position and preparation are key. When your opponents are near the baseline and you have control of the net, pinch the middle with your positioning. Smart players who hit the ball hard know that the middle of the court is the high percentage shot because of the lower net height. They also know that they can create confusion and eliminate hitting balls wide by attacking the middle of the court. Don't give them this luxury!

If the ball is being hit from near the baseline and toward one corner, each defending player should shift toward that side while anticipating a shot hit at or between them. If your opponent can rip a hard crosscourt winner, applaud politely and hope they keep trying that low percentage shot.

Defending hard-hit balls when you are in the mid-court area (no man's land) demands that you keep your body and paddle low. Smart players know to hit aggressive shots at your feet when they can. Put yourself in position to short-hop a "push" shot back into the kitchen, then follow it in.

It's essential to stay connected to your partner on the court. In dinking rallies, shuffle together toward the direction of the opposing hitter to cover the court and eliminate holes that your opponents can exploit. Never remain back in the court when your partner moves forward. Again, you and your partner should move together, playing at the same depth with an emphasis on pinching the middle of the court.

If no matter how you try, you have a shaky backhand groundstroke, position yourself to the left as you get ready to receive serve if you're a right-hander, making it more difficult for your opponent to attack your weaker side.

Finally, scout your opponents. If you play with the same people often, learn their tendencies. Everyone has their favorite attacking shots and preferred placement patterns.

Anticipating their favorite moves gives you a decided advantage, often allowing you to turn defense into offense.

⚙ Communication

News flash! Pickleball is almost always a team game. In addition to chatting about what to have for lunch between points, why not communicate during points as well. On any ball hit down the middle, a calm but firm, "Mine" or "Yours" takes no effort and results in no collisions or confusion as well. On a lob, one player should make the call as well—usually the faster player with the best angle to the ball.

On a third shot drop, I recommend the player not hitting the shot move slightly forward in the court, looking to the side at their partner. If it's a good drop, the hitter says something to the effect of "Yes" or "Go". As they execute the shot, their weight is moving slightly forward. By the time their partner hears "Go" and reacts, this head start position in the court enables the team to move together at the same time. If the drop shot floats high, the hitter can say "No" (or "Uh-oh!"). Their partner now has time to shuffle back and assume a defensive position.

Good communication makes the hitter feel comfortable about executing the shot without any interference, knowing their partner is out of the way and in position to cover the court on the next shot.

⚙ One Thing Leads to Another

I hear a familiar refrain from many of my students: "We practice dinking all the time but when we get in the games, we're mainly just hitting the ball hard at each other. The point is over right away, and we don't get to use our dinks."

Pickleball is a sequential game. Every shot in the rally depends on the quality of the previous shot. A good return of serve forces a third shot from deep in the court. *A good third shot drop forces your opponent to hit up on the ball with less pace on the fourth shot (a dink!), which allows you to take position at the net for the fifth shot (another dink!).* Voila... you are now in a dink game until someone makes an error or can take advantage of a poor dink and hit a power shot.

When you watch top players do their thing, you'll see a ton of dinking. Why? *Because of the quality of their drop shots.* A good third shot drop or reset forces the other player to hit up on the ball with less pace, or risk making an unforced error. If you want to play like the pros, you must become a drop shot *artiste*. Otherwise, the ball you hit high from deep in the court will get pummeled and the point will soon be over as you stand helplessly back near the baseline.

Again, the drop shot sets in motion a sequence of events that results in all players arriving at the kitchen line, using their dinks to move the other team around until an error or winner ensues. This is fun pickleball! However, until you develop a quality drop shot and follow it to the net, you will forever be in "Pickleball Purgatory", whacking at the ball and hoping to get lucky. And remember, if one or both of your opponents are deep in the court, there's no need for a drop shot. Hit it deep to their feet to retain your positional advantage.

Mastering the drop shot is the key that unlocks all the fun shots you can play at the kitchen line. Focus your efforts on this one skill and watch the quality of your game soar.

⊛ The Mental Game

> The game is 90% mental; the
> other half is physical.
>
> ~ *Yogi Berra*

Now that we have covered the shots and the common elements that make every shot more effective, there's only one thing standing between you and pickleball greatness (or at least "above-averageness"). That thing lives inside your head. Without a solid mental game, you can find yourself unable to hit the right shots at the right time. Your decision-making can either sabotage your talent or take it to the next level. And without the right perspective and attitude, even an excellent player will feel unhappy, self-judgmental, and eventually burn out on the game.

Ironically, when you only focus on winning, you lose focus on *what it takes* to win. Winning depends on many variables outside your control—your partner, your opponents, wind, luck... Doing what it takes to win is all that is within your control. When you focus on the concepts below, winning takes care of itself. Or it doesn't. Either way, when you prepare well and play percentage pickleball, you can be satisfied with your effort and accepting of the outcome.

⊛ Shot Selection/Intention

Remember that there are basically two types of shots: "push" shots and "hit" shots. The techniques are quite different, so it's essential to learn both skills and have a clear intention of which one to use as the ball comes to you. Without this clarity, you may find yourself just hitting at the ball, trying to get it over the net without regard for placement or pace. When this happens, you hit balls that sit up and ask to be drilled at you or, even worse, your partner.

Intention can be practiced. Focus on committing to the shot you want to make as soon as possible during a point, even thinking "push" or "hit" as you approach the ball. Eventually, you will integrate this thinking into your game. Unconscious competence comes when your shots are dependable, *and* your intention is clear. Only then are you able to hit the proper shot at the right time to the right location. When you do this consistently, you experience the joy of pickleball!

Shot selection is one part of the decision-making process. Shot placement is the other factor. Remember that placement can beat power. When in doubt, hitting low at the feet of your opponents or between them is the winning decision.

⊙ Patience and Percentages

Patience is a virtue in life—and on the court as well. Set up your points by keeping the ball low and un-attackable until the right time comes. Don't be overeager and try to attack that ball at or below your knees. Keep calm and wait for the ball that comes to you at hip level or above.

Play the percentages. Placement and patience are two aspects of playing high percentage pickleball. Playing smart is very rewarding, especially when you can out-think or out-strategize more physically gifted or younger opponents. In fact, I asked quite a few pickleball veterans and pros to give me their top tips for playing well. The overwhelming top answers were:

1. *Don't attack too soon. Place the ball to force your opponent into an error, then pounce on the higher percentage shot.*
2. *Master the third shot drop.*
3. *Winning is more about reducing unforced errors and keeping the ball un-attackable than about trying to hit winners.*

One other fun tip on playing smart, "percentage" pickleball is to not "Feed the Bear". Everyone you play has their favorite shots. It's fun (and effective) to figure out what those are and not give them what they want. In general, most players are stronger with their forehands and prefer balls that sit up to be whacked. Instead, look for opportunities to keep the ball low, at their feet, and to their backhand. In particular, I'm always looking for an opportunity to hit to the backhand foot on dinks and drops. When I return serve against a banger, I try to hit to their backhand, which is usually their weaker stroke. After all, bears are cute, unless you give them a paddle and allow them to ruin your pickleball picnic...

Don't feed the bear!

⊛ Disguise and Deception

As your game improves, play around with the concepts of disguise and deception. Set your paddle face in one direction, then change it at the last moment to redirect your shot. You can look one way and hit another. When your opponents are back in the court, occasionally pose for an overhead then drop the ball into the kitchen.

One of the best ways to incorporate deception in your pickleball game is to make your set-up for different shots look the same until the last second. For example, when you set up for a simple forehand dink with your paddle in front of you, a quick cock of the wrist enables you to flick the ball at the upper body of the player across from you at the net. By not giving away your intention by taking a backswing or tensing up, you can completely surprise the other player. From this same forehand dink position, you can also lift a lob over the backhand shoulder of your opponent by simply sweeping up on the ball. Again, practice not giving away any clues as to your intention by changing your posture or set-up.

Video #8: DECEPTION AND AGGRESSION AT THE KITCHEN
Watch this video now at https://www.mikebranon.com/joy

In addition to being effective, when you pull off a deceptive shot, you add another element of fun to the game. These techniques keep your opponents off balance and are great to play around with as long as you don't outsmart yourself, get too tricky, and miss too many shots.

◉ Practice

It's a funny thing, the more I
practice, the luckier I get.

~ Arnold Palmer

I hope you have found my physical and mental tips to be helpful. But keep in mind that every technique requires practice to integrate fully into your game. Only when you consistently put in the effort can you say, "I feel like I'm getting the most out of my ability." Then you can be free from stressing about being a world champion and get on with enjoying wherever it is you are.

The aim is to develop muscle memory and mental habits that become second nature instead of requiring constant thinking. Too much thinking on the court can cause you to play mechanically or indecisively. Repetition on the practice court transforms your strokes into automatic (non-thinking), repeatable patterns. Then you are free to focus on strategy and shot selection. In time, even that part of your game becomes automatic. Tension and indecision are reduced because your body is not busy processing constant directions from the mind.

For top players, all parts of the game coalesce, and they experience being in "the zone" or "flow state". But again, Pickleball Nirvana is a rare thing. Most of us must be content with our progress even if we fall short of dominating the top court on a regular basis. You can still find fulfillment in doing your best and enjoying wherever you are on your pickleball journey. At the end of the day, your happiness on the court comes down to attitude.

⊛ A Winning Attitude

I've seen some strange things on pickleball courts... players having an absolute blast—dancing, wearing costumes, singing, and laughing. There was even some guy at a pickleball bachelor party playing while chomping on chips from his pocket while drinking a beer (that might have been me). Many of us are part of competitive groups who love the adrenaline and intensity of high-level play. Others of us are competitive but prioritize the experience of simply being with friends and enjoying the day.

One of my older, wiser students recently told me, "I've won when I step on the court." Consider what "winning" looks like to you. A winning attitude doesn't just mean winning games. *Winning is fun, but fun goes beyond winning.* No matter what skill level you attain, your attitude on the court ultimately determines your happiness level. And I'd rather win at the happiness game than any other game. Here are a couple of tips from a fellow old-timer to make your pickleball experience less stressful and more enjoyable.

⊛ Manage Expectations

In life, unhappiness can be measured as the difference between what we expect and what actually happens. In pickleball, unrealistic expectations can make a fun game an exercise in frustration. If you expect that you will rarely miss shots and hold yourself to unrealistic standards, you're setting yourself up for failure and frustration.

If you have rarely or never played racquet sports, it takes time to build your "kinetic chain"—the footwork and sequencing of your swing. Even if you have played other sports, pickleball is like anything else in life—it's not a predictable, smooth ride to the top. But predictable things can become boring. Embrace your personal pickleball journey with realistic expectations and enjoy the ride.

⊛ Find Your Tribe

Your happiness on the court depends on those around you. I guarantee you will not be happy if you are either easily dominating every game or constantly getting your butt kicked. Attitude can only take you so far. Find your tribe that meshes with your skill level and attitude. It may take some time, but when you find your Pickleball Posse, life is good!

⊕ Let It Go

Not just a hit song from *Frozen*. . . darn good advice for playing well and playing happy.

WE ALL MISS!!!

Some misses are worse than others. Raise your hand if you've ever whiffed an overhead and had it bounce off your head. Or brilliantly angled your opponent out of position, only to flub an easy shot to a wide-open court. Or hit a crappy lob right to your opponent at the net and watched your partner go into the fetal position as the ball rockets off their backside. (Is it just me?)

When you miss an easy shot, it's okay to experience a flash of anger or disappointment—we're only human. (Just try to keep the F-bombs, self-flagellation, and paddle throwing to a minimum.) But then it's time to clear your head and move on to the next point. Missing is not a character flaw, it just happens sometimes no matter how beautiful, charming, and talented you are. If you have a bad day, smile anyway, and keep those other players wondering how wonderful the rest of your life must be.

Many of my students will hit several solid shots during drills or a point, but when they eventually miss, they focus on the miss and forget all the good shots and progress they are making. The same thing happens to us off the court. . . we focus on the negative news and discount the generosity and kindness all around us. Practice giving more attention to the positive things and gently nudging the negative aside—on and off the court.

If someone irritates you during a game, shrug it off. As wonderful as pickleball and its players are, we have members of our pickleball family who are not fun to be around.

Bite your lip and move on to another game. There's enough conflict in the world without adding to it on the pickleball court. Hang out with the 97.3% of the good folks you see each day* and don't let missed shots define who you are and ruin your day. Let it go.

⬤ Negative Self-Talk

"How could you do that?"
"What an idiot!"
"You suck!"
No, that's not someone watching a politician on TV from that "other" party (at least not this time...). It's the brutal self-analysis we sometimes hear on the pickleball court—and that's just the audible dialogue. The internal criticism can be even worse.

We love to compete, but scathing self-criticism doesn't help. It makes other players cringe and hurts your level of

---

* I undertook a painstaking statistical analysis of players and found that 97 out of 100 were really cool, two need extensive therapy, and one just needs to have their coffee before playing. Not a bad percentage overall...

play. Remember, you're hitting a plastic ball around with your friends at this stage of life. How could you not be grateful for that?

Reasonable expectations, a short memory, self-compassion, and gratitude make you a winner on the court no matter what the score. And life is more pleasant when you apply that mindset off the court as well.

⊛ Putting It All Together

I've given you my best advice to play well and play happy. However, no matter how concise and to the point I try to be, it's hard to integrate a lot of information and use it instantly when the ball is flying at you. That's why it's best to focus on one thing at a time. Decide each day you play what your emphasis will be. Keeping the paddle square to your target? Early preparation? Hitting to the feet? Being kind to yourself and others? As time goes on, these aspects of your game will feel more natural, and you will move toward unconscious competence—the zone where good play flows more naturally without conscious thinking.

I have given you a lot of information on playing better, but as I mentioned at the beginning of the book, sometimes less is more. So, let's narrow our focus and summarize the key concepts that enable you to bring the right skill set and mindset to the court every day.

⦿ PHYSICAL KEYS

As you get older, a dedication to *pre-shot preparation, shot placement, and proper fundamentals* are the weapons at your disposal to make up for a relative lack of power, reflexes, or mobility.

Again, I want to stress that we don't become instantly feeble on our 50th or 75th birthday. There's still plenty of gas in our tanks to play an aggressive, physical game. However, these principles will benefit your game at any age, and at some point, when we eventually slow down a bit, this brand of pickleball ages well.

⦿ STRATEGIC KEYS

Pickleball strategy is a topic that could fill an entire book on its own. Take lessons and explore other resources to develop the strategic side of your game. In the meantime, focus on the following concepts to play your best:

Play at the kitchen line. Keep your opponents under pressure, back in the court, and off balance. Have a *clear intention* of where and how you want to hit the ball. *Keep the ball low*, avoiding the power zones of your opponents (don't feed the bear). Strive to *play patiently* and error-free. When you're at the kitchen, hit low balls soft and low over the net. Attack balls at waist level or above. Make the third shot drop a vital part of your game.

⦿ PSYCHOLOGICAL KEYS

Practice being happy on the court. Shrug off mistakes, celebrate good play by you and others, compliment freely, and *play with gratitude*. Never lose sight of the fact that life and pickleball are meant to be enjoyed. Part of that enjoyment comes from having the right attitude, but there's no denying that making every effort to play well and win is also an immense source of happiness. When you play well and play happy, you are maximizing your pickleball experience.

If you are trying to improve your game, I commend you. Because we're best pickleball buddies by now, I have broken down all the pickleball advice in the universe even further into the following 10 Commandments. Take a right at the Burning Bush and look for the old guy in the faded tank top holding stone tablets with a pickleball bag slung over his shoulder.

⊚ Pickleball 10 Commandments

1. Keep your paddle and both hands up at the net, ready for a hard shot. **Make ball-to-paddle contact in front of you.**
2. Move your feet quickly to get in the proper hitting position, get balanced, and contact the ball **with a paddle face that is square to your target.**
3. Have **a clear intention** on each shot as the ball approaches you. Practice shot selection. Push or hit the ball as the situation dictates. Don't settle for mindlessly hitting and hoping.
4. **Get to the kitchen line.** That is where most points are won. When making your way to the kitchen line: Pause, Hit It Low, Move Forward.
5. When dinking or hitting drop shots: **Low, Set, Push.**

6. **Play low!** Keep the ball low and to the backhand foot to avoid being attacked (especially when playing bangers). Keep your body low in an athletic position with weight on the balls of your feet.

7. When you're cookin' at the kitchen, **hit low balls soft. Hit high balls hard.**

8. Make the **third shot drop** a dependable part of your game.

9. **Accelerate through the ball** with a short backswing and longer follow-through.

10. **Be patient.** Work the ball around until you are set up to go for a winner.

⊙ Special Bonus Commandment: HAVE FUN!!!

(If you're smiling and laughing, you're winning, no matter what the score.)

PLAYING HEALTHIER

THE ONLY THING WORSE THAN PLAY-ing poorly is not playing at all.

Like anything else that's fun and addictive, enjoy pickleball in moderation. Make sure you don't play so much that your body can't handle the strain. Listen to your body and be careful of overdoing it. Mix in stretching and low-impact cardio to keep that machine running well. After all, we're all running around in what amounts to used cars with a lot of mileage on them. Take care of that vintage beauty and you can keep playing for a good, long time.

Pickleballs usually don't do much harm. You may get a bruise or a bloody lip if you're unlucky, but the main thing to watch out for is getting hit in the eye. Trust me, I know from experience. I took a pickleball directly to my unprotected eye and now have permanent damage to my vision. (The good news is that I have a great excuse when I miss!) But seriously, wear sport goggles or sunglasses and you're good to go.

The only other equipment advice I have is to find proper court shoes and a paddle that suit *your* needs. With shoes, find the brand that provides support and comfort. Foot injuries can derail your pickleball plans in a heartbeat.

Well... at least they're wearing protective eyewear and proper court shoes...*

With paddles, find the feel and weight that suit you best and doesn't cause elbow or wrist pain. Heavier paddles can provide more power, whereas lighter paddles are easier to maneuver and can improve your touch. If you're new to the game, start with a paddle in the $50–$90 range, then upgrade once you find out what feels right to you. (No wood paddles, please... there are plenty of inexpensive paddles that are appropriate for this century.) If something isn't working, demo

---

* Naked Pickleball, posted in *Apparel, Growing Pickleball, Places to Play* by *Anna*. From Pickleball Central.com Blog 7/25/13

a different paddle until you find one that works for you. Just don't switch paddles constantly because you think it will fix your game. It might help, but top players can win playing with a frying pan.

⊙ Embrace Exercise

One of my favorite books is *Younger Next Year.* It makes a compelling case for exercise as the key to health. It states that after age 50, our bodies start to decay, losing muscle mass and flexibility (exciting, right?). Exercise promotes cellular repair and renewal as well as releasing dopamine that makes us feel happy and energized. When you exercise, you actively enhance the quality of your life—it's the secret to successful aging.

According to the doctor who co-wrote the book, you should exercise six days a week for the rest of your life. No excuses. No negotiations. Doctor's orders!

> The keys to overriding the decay code are
> daily exercises, emotional commitment,
> reasonable nutrition, and a real engagement
> with living. But it starts with exercise. Aging
> is up to nature, but decay is up to you.
> *~ Younger Next Year*

Pickleball checks all these boxes (except for nutrition... you'll have to put down the donut and tackle that one on your own).

We know that movement is essential for cardiovascular health. We also know that when we move, sometimes we fall down and go boom. To counteract these possibilities, always stretch before and after you play. Make sure to get your heart pumping by warming up beforehand.

And remember, don't backpedal to get balls hit over your head—let your partner run (or if they're "life experienced", amble) at an angle to retrieve the ball. Play within your abilities to avoid injury. Don't be a Pickleball Hero for one shining moment and end up on the sidelines for several dull weeks.*

⊙ Prepare Your Body

To improve your odds of playing healthily and playing well, build your cardio, strength, and flexibility prior to embarking on your quest to be world (or retirement community) champion. Pickleball-specific exercises should target cardio, agility, balance, core strength, and lower body strength.

- Your cardiovascular fitness improves your pickleball. And your pickleball improves your cardio. Don't you just love win-win scenarios? When you make cardio a priority, you get to more balls and can play longer at a higher level.

- For agility, practice shuffle steps and quick change of direction moves after warming up and before you

---

* OK, maybe I'm not the right person to tell you this as I tend to run into things and have been known to chase pickleballs like an Aussie Shephard, exhibiting a similar IQ (my apologies to Aussie Shepherds).

play. You can also do drills that focus on quick move-
ments in the dink game and proper footwork such as
split-steps as you move from the baseline area to the
kitchen.

- For balance, yoga poses are very helpful. Proper balance results in better shot-making. It also makes for
fewer falls on and off the court. Falls are the most
common injury for people over 65, according to the
CDC. Improved balance and movement from playing
pickleball enhances your overall health.

- Core strength is especially important for the twisting
moves you make on the court. A strong core helps keep
your back healthy, supporting your more fragile lower
back and hip areas. (We may not be able to rock that
six-pack anymore, but we can stay strong underneath
those groceries we're carrying around.)

- Squats and lunges strengthen your lower body and
enable you to maintain a low, balanced posture as you
play. Whole-body resistance exercises keep your bones
and muscles functioning well and enable you to play
more powerfully.

If necessary, find a personal trainer to gently encourage
or whip you into shape depending on your goals. Every sport
depends on a sound body, especially as we age. Prepare yours
properly and you'll play better, healthier, and happier. And
that's what we're all here to do.

There are two videos on my website that can help you stay
flexible and reduce the chance of injury. The first one (Mike's

Morning Stretch) demonstrates my morning stretch routine, which can be done in less than 10 minutes. It's a combination of easy yoga and stretching. After experiencing severe back problems in my younger years, this routine has played a big part in keeping me almost pain-free for many years.

Many people don't stretch because they have trouble making time for it in their busy lives. Personally, I believe taking care of yourself should rank somewhere above getting irritated for hours on end by politicians as you read the news, or obsessively checking Facebook to see who "liked" that picture of your burrito combo from dinner yesterday. For those who disagree, my second video (Better Back/Happier Hamstrings) is a simple series of moves that can take you zero extra minutes a day to do. How is that possible? Well, you can do these moves while leaning comfortably against a table, couch, or desk while you're on your computer or watching TV. You get a great stretch in your legs, hips, and lower back even as you shake your head at the news or watch videos of clumsy cats. (You can also do these stretches while leaning casually against a net post or fence at the court before you play as you talk about strategy or that guy with the neon shorts and the "I Have a Dinking Problem" t-shirt on Court #3.)

No matter what you do to stay healthy, any sport, especially as we get older, involves a degree of risk. Pickleball is no exception. Our generation is among the first to fully commit to exercise and movement as a lifestyle. Twenty years ago, if you brought up pickleball, Peloton, and yoga pants, people would have shuffled away quietly, avoiding eye contact. Today, it's perfectly normal to whack plastic balls at each other, jump on a stationary bike while a stranger 3000 miles away hollers at you on a video screen, and see 60-year-old hotties rocking the Lululemon gear.

Talk with any experienced (old) player before you hit the court and ask them how their body is doing. Chances are they will have more than one nagging injury or trouble spot to tell you about. It's part of the deal we make when we push our older bodies to perform. But it's a deal we make willingly. It beats the alternative of sitting on a bench and watching the world go by.

⊙ Warming Up

Congratulations! You embraced exercise and upped your strength and flexibility. You're a pickleball machine! Then you hop out of your car, saunter over to the court, dink for two minutes, and yell, "Game on!" Five minutes into the game, you run up for a drop shot, and "Yowww!"

When you show up to play, develop a warmup routine and stick to it. Your routine should consist of these four categories:

1. **Movement/Cardio**
   Literally warm up your body and get oxygen pumping through your system. Walk briskly, skip around on the balls of your feet, and get the blood flowing to those body parts that were snoring quietly while you were drinking coffee and sending emails.

2. **Joint rotation**

Rotate your ankles, knees, hips, and shoulders in both directions. This action lubricates your joints with synovial fluid that acts like oil in an engine, allowing your bones to move past one another more smoothly.

3. **Stretching**

   Stretching loosens your muscles for the demands you are about to make on them. Feel free to use or modify my Morning Stretch and Back/Hamstring routines or come up with one that best meets your needs.

4. **Pickleball-specific movement**

   Standing flat-footed and dinking for a couple of minutes neither warms you up nor prepares you to play well. Move side to side, dink crosscourt, exchange groundstrokes, groove some third shot drops, and volley back and forth quickly at the net. Prepare yourself to hit every shot while acclimating your body to the moves you are about to make at full speed.

When you establish a habitual warmup routine, not only do you reduce the risk of injury, but you also play better. Your body will be loose and ready to perform. Remember, the only thing worse than playing poorly is not being able to play at all.

The Big Picture: Risks and Rewards

Now that you know some of the risks, and my lawyer says I'm off the hook, let's look at some compelling physical and mental health benefits of playing pickleball. In fact, here's some stuff from folks with PhDs. I'm sure I know more than they do, but I guess they went to "school" and are "smart". Just remember, I'm a PhD too (Pretty Happy Dude), so who do you really trust?

Pickleball Benefit #1: You'll Lower Your Risk of Heart Disease
A recent study in the International Journal of Research in Exercise Physiology found middle-aged and older adults who played one hour of pickleball three days per week for six weeks improved their blood pressure, cholesterol, and cardiorespiratory fitness levels.

Pickleball Benefit #2: You'll Cut Your Risk of Depression
Exercise in general is a proven mood booster—and pickleball is no exception. A recent study in *Leisure Studies* found older adults who played in pickleball tournaments had a lower risk of depression. (I would guess that this benefit applies to non-tournament players as well.)

"I believe it makes older adults' lives richer and happier," says study author, Jungsu Ryu, PhD, an assistant professor of sport management at Marshall University. "Engaging seriously in playing pickleball may buffer any type of negative emotions that people have during transitions to retirement and later life."

Pickleball Benefit #3: You'll Get Hooked on Exercise
A study in the *Journal of Aging and Physical Activity* found people become loyal to the sport because it helps them meet

their fitness goals and enhance social connections. It's a two-for-one workout!

"Sometimes people are more willing to play a sport when it's fun, and people report that playing pickleball is way more fun than going for a walk or going on the treadmill," says Jonathan Casper, PhD, the study author. "If you were to spend 60 minutes in the gym," he continues, "it usually feels like 60 minutes. But when you're doing something you enjoy, like pickleball, where you typically have time to talk and laugh in the game, all of a sudden, you've been playing for 60 minutes and you think, 'Where did the time go?'"

Pickleball Benefit #4: You'll Socialize More—and Feel Less Lonely

Pickleball is a great social outlet. And that desire to connect with friends will keep you coming back again and again. "There's this fun aspect, which really ties into social support," says Chris Gagliardi, a spokesperson for the American Council on Exercise.

Even while on the court, interactions between pickleball players are different from those in other physical activities, Casper says. "Because this is a sport with two people playing together, you have that engagement," he says. "And people are so passionate about pickleball—they look for opportunities to show other people and share their enjoyment. *That's more so with pickleball than any other sport that I've studied.*"

Pickleball Benefit #5: You May Stay Independent Longer

Older adults who play pickleball regularly can improve their reflexes and balance, which can help you live independently for longer, Gagliardi says. You may also improve your range of motion, which can help minimize arthritis symptoms that prevent you from performing everyday tasks with ease. "As a result of not being physically active, you typically lose range of motion," Gagliardi says. "If you're doing something you enjoy, you're more likely to do it. But also, with pickleball, you have to think about the strategy and the hand-eye coordination," he explains. "If you're sedentary, you're not doing that at all."*

⊛ Dealing with Limitations

Even when you do everything right, injuries can still happen. Some days it feels like a full-time job managing our creaky, achy bodies. Backs, hips, knees, and shoulders seem to be the common trouble spots for older pickleball players. Anti-inflammatories, braces, and physical therapy can help us cope, but sometimes our joints just wear down after all the hard miles we've put on them. Every pickleball addict's nightmare is being stuck at home after an injury or surgery, itching to get back in the game. (And every pickleball spouse's nightmare is that muttering, grumpy so-and-so on their couch. . .)

If you love sports, you will probably be back playing before you're 100%. By all means, don't rush it. Listen to your body (and your doctor) if you want to avoid setbacks. But the good news is that there are ways to ease back into the game and compensate for your current lack of mobility. These tips also

---

* Excerpts from. . . *5 Hidden Health Benefits of Pickleball* By Lisa Fields | March 26, 2019

apply if you are permanently limited by your footspeed as you get older.

For example, it's essential to get from the service line to the kitchen line ASAP, especially after a service return. This can be challenging if your body can no longer get out of first gear or if you are dragging a bum foot, knee, or hip along with you. So, what do you do?

For the service return, hit the ball on a high arc and deep crosscourt. By lofting instead of driving the ball, you give yourself more time to get to the kitchen. By returning crosscourt, your partner can now protect you by covering the middle as you transition forward. Try it! And enjoy your leisurely stroll to the kitchen.

Another technique is to move up to the ball and short-hop it with your service return or groundstroke. This allows you to move forward at contact, reducing the distance to the kitchen for your next shot. Less steps take less time.

The same thing applies to third shots. If you can't move quickly, avoid driving the ball from deep in the court, which leaves you stuck at the back line when your opponent volleys back deep to you. Instead, plan on 2-3 low drop shots, working your way forward until you reach the kitchen line. Once there, your lack of mobility doesn't matter as much, and you can rely on your usual, magnificent net game!

What makes pickleball so fun and interesting are the many tactics that can accomplish the same mission. Whether you are temporarily or permanently limited by your movement, there are strategies that enable you to play smart and effectively. You can still find ways to enjoy the game, which brings us to my last piece of advice:

Play for fun all the time... but especially when injured or rehabilitating.

Consider playing below your normal level. Many of those players will be thrilled to play with you and you will have less stress and more fun as you play your way back into shape. Rediscover the joy of playing without having to grind hard and push your limits on every point. Learn to let the tough ball go and practice saying, "Nice shot!". Take it easy and look forward to the day when you can play your best again. Soon, you'll be the one hearing "nice shot" from your friends once again.

Pickleball: Part of a Balanced Diet

One of the reasons we need to know how to cope with limitations is that we can become _truly_ addicted to this game. Some evenings, my wife will watch me hobble around the house after a full day of playing and coaching, shake her head, give me "the look", and ask, "You're playing tomorrow, right?" Of course, the answer is almost always "Yes". Once I stretch and get moving the next day, pop an ibuprofen or two, and see my friends, I'm ready to go. But I have come to realize that this behavior isn't sustainable or healthy.

As much as I hate to make concessions to age, my body needs more recovery time these days. So does my mind. I don't want to rain on your Pickleball Parade but there's more to life than swatting a plastic ball around (horrified gasp from the crowd!). As a former massage therapist, I recall seeing many clients who suffered from repetitive stress syndrome, whether it was sitting behind a desk for 50 hours a week, driving a truck, or playing a demanding sport.

It's never fun to turn down requests to play, but we all need to recharge physically and mentally. By all means, keep moving and interacting, but mix it up a bit. Make time for resistance training, stretching, and light cardio so that you stay strong and balanced. Read a good book, travel without your paddle, and recharge your battery by pursuing those things that used to fill your days before pickleball pushed them aside.

We're supposed to be older *AND* wiser. Know when to say "No". Give yourself a break and feel revitalized the next time you join your friends on the court.

PLAYING HAPPIER

I'S GREAT TO GET CONFIRMATION from doctors and researchers that pickleball can be very good for you. If you already play, you know how this game makes you feel. However, to get even more out of your pickleball experience, let's dig a little deeper and ponder what underlies the happiness you feel when you whack a shot past your buddies or have a beverage with them afterward.

The following topics explore the optimal attitude on the court, potential psychological roadblocks, and group dynamics. I encourage you to contemplate different ways of viewing your time on the court that go beyond who gets to 11 first, and see the game as an opportunity to integrate the way you play pickleball with the way you live your life.

⚙ Growth Mindset

A growth mindset may be the single most important quality you can develop to make any stage of your life, especially your senior years, more fulfilling. As we age, we might shut down and close ourselves off a bit. Loneliness can creep into our lives. Nurturing our growth mindset enables us to say yes to life, persevere, and embrace the challenge of living fully at any age.

Pickleball is an opportunity to reawaken and engage with your world. It encourages you to improve your fitness, learn new techniques, and employ strategies to outwit your opponents. It's a puzzle you never finish, but that's what keeps you coming back, determined to play your best and get the most out of every game and every day.

⚙ The Good Life

Of course, unless you dream of becoming a pro, pickleball is mainly to be enjoyed. It's great playing with people who can laugh at themselves, give compliments freely, and support their partners even when they miss easy shots. We may not remember the scores, but we sure do remember how it is to play with someone who is pleasant and supportive... or the opposite. Pickleball is an opportunity to hone your social skills, develop a positive attitude, and savor every single day.

Between points, occasionally take a moment to look around and listen:

You'll see your fellow players moving and hustling around the court. You'll also see smiles and the simple joy of playing with others. You'll hear hurried footsteps, pickleballs popping off paddles, and shouts of disappointment or exultation. You'll also hear laughter and good-natured conversation as you would at a happy family gathering. And make no mistake... when you're with the right people, a happy family is exactly what pickleball feels like. And who doesn't want more of that feeling in their life?

Life is good on the pickleball court.

◌ Competitive Leisure

Some of us miss our highly competitive days, whether it involved business or sports. Back in the day, many of us were highly focused on carving out our niche in the world—striving and acquiring were our default motivations. Yet we never completely lose the evolutionary imperative to compete, even if it's mahjong or shuffleboard. And that's great! Competition keeps us feeling young and vital.

Yet our wise self now sees this urge in the context of our current situation. The stakes just aren't as high anymore. We compete because we enjoy the feeling, not because of some urgent compulsion.

*Our reality is competitive leisure,
which is the best of both worlds.*

The aches and pains of getting older aren't much fun, but studies show that older people are generally happier than those beautiful young, obsessed folks who get all the attention. We may occasionally feel invisible, but we're more comfortable in our own (somewhat wrinkled and dry) skin.

Pickleball embodies the concept of competitive leisure. It's accessible and fun, yet challenging enough to get the adrenaline flowing again. Even if you're ripping a ball past somebody's great-grandmother, just pretend that she's a superstar athlete and let that fist-pump happen!

⊕ Serious Fun

How do you define fun? Is it winning a gold medal at a big tournament or simply playing with your friends?

The concept of "serious fun" means that you can dive into this sport, work hard, practice, and hone your skills—becoming the best player you can be and experiencing the rush of competition from younger days. However, it also means that you are free to find your own place in the game, never losing sight of the fact that fun is what makes pickleball so special. Competing is fun in and of itself, but not at the cost of failing to enjoy your time on the court with good friends. The laughter and camaraderie ultimately mean more than winning at this stage of life.

There's nothing wrong with other sports and activities; golf, tennis, and good old walking are wonderful ways to compete, connect, or stay active, but pickleball is unique. It gets under your skin and gives a lighthearted purpose to your days. Many of you already realize that the path from your first dink to pickleball addiction is a slippery slope. And it's a healthy addiction—the desire to learn new skills, get your body moving, and meet great people.

⊛ Competition Therapy

As you get older, you might miss those days of competitive sports—or maybe you never had the opportunity to compete and now is your time. Those of you with years of competition under your belt remember lessons learned on how to compete the right way, developing skills that enriched other parts of your life. Pickleball gives you the chance to once again feel the surge of adrenaline that competition brings. Yes, the social aspects of the game are wonderful, but when you're out on the court, especially as your level of play improves, it's exciting and rewarding to try to outwit and outplay your opponents.

The key to enjoying competitive pickleball is understanding the process of learning and improving. Be patient along the way as you navigate the "stages of competence" I discussed earlier, but look to speed up the process and increase your enjoyment of the game by getting proper instruction and practicing with a purpose.

One of the rewards of working hard on your game is the feeling of being in "the zone", focused, and completely in charge. All your problems and mental noise must sit quietly on the sidelines while you're engaged in the present moment.

I call this "competition therapy". When the game is over, you tap paddles, appreciative of the spirit of competition and sportsmanship. The glow of playing your best stays with you and the rest of your day feels that much better.

⊛ Finding You're Enough

Striving to improve is an important aspect of sports. But beware of becoming so driven that the joy of playing is lost along the way. Consider this. . . striving to improve is an important aspect of *life*. But beware of becoming so driven that the joy of *living* is lost along the way.

Pause occasionally to contemplate if the desire to improve is actually making you miserable. There are enough outside voices in the marketing and social media world telling you that you need to have more and be more to be truly happy. When your inner voice buys into this, you can never be satisfied.

Also, remember to be patient with yourself and not get caught in the "comparison trap", feeling less because others are better. When you notice a better player, you can't help but wish you could do what they seem to do effortlessly. Even though pickleball courts are pretty level, it's not a level playing field. Some players have extensive tennis backgrounds or incredible hand-eye coordination or are young and good-looking. If they have it all, then yes, resent them deeply (just kidding. . .). Instead, feel free to admire great talent and get right back to enjoying who you are and what you can do. Your friends (and your dog) think you're pretty cool just as you are.

The happiest players (and people) I know exude a sense of contentment—they may get frustrated temporarily but quickly return to their true, wise selves. Accept that there are limits to your mastery of pickleball (and life). "Finding you're enough" is embracing the apparent conflict of being content and the desire to improve. *The quest to improve doesn't mean throwing yourself away and becoming a new person—it's an opportunity to embrace who you are already and open yourself to new and interesting experiences.*

⊙ Etiquette

Although we are generally a kind, well-adjusted crowd, occasionally, issues arise that can ruin a good time. How do you deal with sticky situations on the court?

Like anything else in life, you may not get along great with everyone, but you can usually find a group that fits you. If you get stuck with a partner who is relatively unskilled, just work on your game, stay positive, and move along to the next game. This usually happens during open play where diverse players congregate. It's frustrating to put your paddle in line and wait 20 minutes or more, only to match up with a player who has no business playing at the level of the game. You lose 11-1 and proceed to sit again until God knows when. The only solution is to set up private games when you can. Otherwise, you must make peace with the open play lottery.

When playing an opponent who can't move well in a recreational game, try not to lob them when they are at the kitchen or hit drop shots when they're at the baseline unless you have their permission. And obviously, don't rifle balls at close range at the body or head of someone's Nana or Papa who is just trying to get out and have some fun. Save that treatment for your buddies when you're playing for beers afterward.

What is the proper etiquette when playing a team with one player who is notably worse than the other? In tournament play, unleash your inner predator and attack the weaker player. However, in recreational play, try to spread the ball around. It's no fun for the weaker player to be picked on and it's just as frustrating for their stronger partner to stand around and not hit the ball at all. Besides, what are you trying to prove? Crushing a less talented player won't improve your game. Challenge yourself by trying to outplay the stronger opponent. You'll improve your game and exemplify the proper pickleball ethic in the bargain.

To avoid putting other players in these situations, strive to play in games at or around your own level. It's no fun for you or others when skill levels are too far apart unless everyone understands and accepts the situation ahead of time. Don't be *that guy* who butts into games way above his pay grade or looks for games he can dominate. Seriously, just don't.

Now that we're all playing nice with each other, let's take a deep breath and enjoy. . .

⊕... A Pickleball Namaste

For those of you who are newer to the game, tapping paddles is one of our favorite pickleball customs. This ritual is done at the net when the game is over. Everyone taps paddles and shares a sincere "good game" whether they win or lose. It's like a "Pickleball Namaste"—you acknowledge the effort and good times that you share with your partner and your opponents. It exemplifies the spirit of pickleball—respect and appreciation for everyone in our pickleball community.

⊕ Belonging

Pickleball truly is a community, especially if you frequent a particular club or location. You see the same people most days and play with them as well as against them. If you're an empty nester, it's like finding a new family with all the wisecracking and unique personalities you (mostly) love, without the family drama.

If you are relatively new to the sport, it may take a while to find games and groups with whom you are comfortable. Open play, in which you rotate around, or group clinics are great ways to meet new folks. Rest assured you will eventually find your tribe that meshes with your skill level and personality. Social interaction and activity are key elements of successful aging. It's a true joy to find your pickleball soul mates and look forward to being together as much as possible.

⊙ Ditch the Drama

Belonging to a group is wonderful—dealing with moods and personalities can be exhausting. Be careful to not get caught up in the gossip and sniping that inevitably seep into group dynamics. We don't need to all get along perfectly... we just need to get along. Do your best to overlook occasional odd behaviors in others and hope that they overlook yours.

Unfortunately, some of us got older but never grew up. When someone is unpleasant during open play, be grateful that you only have to deal with them for one game, then move on to greener pastures. You can express your feelings if necessary but the odds of changing someone's personality and habits in a matter of minutes are usually slim.

Addressing a problem with someone in your regular group

is a bit trickier. If you're the only one who has an issue with them, it may be wise for you to find another group. If there's a consensus that a player is getting out of hand, one or more members of the group need to address that individual calmly and rationally. If they are not receptive to change, it's far healthier to disinvite them than have everyone walk on eggshells or dread showing up at all. It's better to rip off the Band-Aid than let one person drag the group down or get caught up in complaining to each other. Then you can get back to why you play pickleball in the first place—enjoying every day on the court with good friends.

⊚ Situational Friendships

Another "Pickleball Plus" is situational friendships. We look forward to seeing and playing with our fellow players. We come together to get away from the real world and have fun with no strings attached. We may socialize occasionally in real life, but often, these friendships are confined to the courts.

This doesn't mean we don't care about each other; it can just be healthy to gravitate together around something as simple and pure as play. In this polarized world, we don't need another occasion to delve into political or social issues. Out here, those topics fade into the background noise (like they used to). We connect as fellow humans, united by our passion for the game and enjoyment of each other. When we're on the court, the only thing that should divide us is a net.

◌ Coping with Failure

Maybe failure is a bit harsh, but coming up short of your expectations is something that everyone must deal with, whether you're a beginner or a pro. You put in time and effort to play your best, but it seems like you keep making the same mistakes and feel like you're not getting any better. Yeah, it's just a game, but you can't help being frustrated when you make mistakes in the short term or fall short of your goals to improve in the long term.

The truth is that most of us are improving if we are putting in the effort by practicing and learning from good coaches. However, improvement is a "two steps up and one step back" process. Some days it's a "one step up and two steps back" slog. For senior players, we also must deal with the gradual erosion of our physical abilities. I'm pretty fast for an old guy, but a friend of mine loves to joke that "Old Mike" would have gotten to that drop shot. Sadly, "Young Mike" probably would have gotten there but "Old Mike" has lost a step.

It's okay to feel frustrated when you miss an easy shot or have a bad day. But this is the nature of challenge—it's challenging! When you practice and compete, you're not accepting the status quo, you're challenging yourself to push past your comfort zone and maximize your talent. That makes you a winner in my book no matter the outcome. Unfortunately, no matter how hard you try and how much you want to win, you will usually lose to better players. Even when playing at your own level, you will play well one day and flub easy shots the next time out.

We would all love to raise our game to another level, make fewer errors, and hear others speak in hushed tones about our mastery of the game. However, playing happier is all about understanding that we're all in the same boat and not letting our misses define who we are and ruin our time on the court. Accept that pickleball is not a game of perfect. Accept that if you are truly challenging yourself, you're not just finding games you can easily win—and that means you will often lose. Accept that improvement is not a straight-line path to perfection. Only then are you free to celebrate the little victories and not let unrealistic expectations ruin your pickleball experience.

Try hard. Have fun. Play nice. These are the only things you can control. Winning and losing just happens along the way.

⊛ Gratitude

Gratitude turns what we have into enough.

~ Aesop*

Pause occasionally during and after games to appreciate your good fortune to be healthy enough to play and compete at your age. I hope that you truly do take time to pause... look

---

* Aesop was a "fabled" Greek pickleball champ, who wrote "The Tortoise and The Hare", a story about a pickleball player who rushed around the court and went for winners every time, who got beat by an older player who set up points, used drop shots, and played patiently.

around... and smile. Too many of us have lost our mobility and independence. Life is finite and health is not guaranteed—you can never be too grateful.

If you're playing pickleball in this crazy, often unfair world, there aren't many people luckier than you. I could ramble on about gratitude until you would just be grateful if I would ever stop. So, instead, I'll hand the microphone to some folks like us who have overcome adversity and exemplify playing with perspective and gratitude.

STORIES

EVERYBODY HAS A STORY. ONE OF the best things in life is hearing the stories of others. Whether I'm traveling or playing pickleball, I often hear personal stories that inspire and amaze me. Quite often, even if we are older, we forget that the person across from us wasn't always old. We're just getting a snapshot from what has often been a fascinating journey. Here are a few of those stories to give you an idea of how pickleball has enriched the lives of so many diverse people.

Paulette found pickleball when she needed it most. Her life had suddenly changed, and she found herself empty-nested. Like many of us, she wanted to fill her time with something that was good for her body and soul, and she craved an outlet for her

Paulette, channeling her inner Tiger Woods

abundant energy... a place where she could find a sense of family again. As she shared, "Pickleball became my refuge."

Paulette is a popular figure at our club, spending countless hours improving her game and helping others improve theirs. She brings healthy, homemade baked goods and runs pickleball drills she found online to both nurture and challenge her new friends. Pickleball has played a significant role in reconnecting her with her innate positivity and love of play—and finding a family when she needed one most.

Rick had recently taken up the game when he moved to the pickleball hotbed of Naples, Florida. Like many of us, it was love at first dink, and he was soon playing 5-6 days a week and enjoying his new friends. Everything was fine until he started losing feeling in his legs as he finished playing one day. Two days later, he couldn't even stand up, went to the hospital, and was in surgery hours later. After the emergency procedure, he awoke to the reality of life in a wheelchair. It was a gut shot to a healthy, active guy.

Fortunately, Rick is a fighter. He threw himself into acute rehab, convincing his therapist to let him hit pickleballs with his weight supported to keep his reflexes and coordination in good order. He also enlisted the support of a local instructor, Joe, who was experienced at playing in a wheelchair. Joe helped him get the equipment and training to play again with some minor rule modifications (he gets two bounces; his front wheels can go into the kitchen but the back ones stay out). He now plays a couple of days a week with a mixed group.

Rick hopes his condition will improve, but in the meantime, he is committed to make the best of a tough situation. And pickleball is his ticket to staying active and connected. When you hear him talk, perspective, gratitude, and determination ooze from his pores. You get the feeling he'll be okay no matter what the future holds.

Paul was a successful businessman and devoted father. When he received a terminal cancer diagnosis, his family wanted to find a way to keep him active and engaged with life during the arduous chemo process. They decided to paint a pickleball court in their driveway during the early days of the pandemic in 2020, moving all their backyard furniture and a fire pit out front to create their own family pickleball club!

It also turned out to be a fun way to engage Paul's five teenage grandchildren and to keep them active amid the closure of schools, sports, and their social lives. The family never realized how pickleball would ultimately give them the irreplaceable gift of togetherness in Paul's final months.

Every birthday and holiday was celebrated in the front yard surrounding the pickleball court at a safe distance, with an excessive amount of sanitizing, and a whole lot of love and laughter. Most days, Paul was too weak to join in, but he would sit on the sidelines and offer his witty and humorous commentary. On occasion, he would stand and steal a paddle from someone nearby, only to hit a few balls before the exhaustion kicked in. Nonetheless, this was where he loved to be—watching his children, grandchildren, and wife of 50 years play and feel joy together.

When he finally succumbed to his battle with cancer on August 28 of 2020, the family was devastated. But in time, they realized that their family patriarch had lived his final days as best as he could. The joy of pickleball still resonates with the family. Paul's daughter, Aubri, has honored her father by founding Civile Apparel, a pickleball clothing line. And every time the family goes out to play, Paul's legacy of love and laughter is all around them.

From a young age, Bill felt alone. He never really found a place to fit in. A few years ago, he attended the US Open Pickleball Championships and was welcomed by a diverse group of people who imparted their love of the game to him. He was inspired to take up the game, and these days, he plays several nights a week in his hometown.

Bill explains how pickleball "saved his life":

> "For the first time in a long time, I feel part of something. I have something to look forward to and, quite honestly, it cured what could simply be called depression. I feel healthier, I can see a difference in my professional life, and I am genuinely happy—for the first time in years.

I'm hopeful that as a lover of pickleball—no matter how skilled you may be—you'll continue to welcome new players, both good and bad, with open arms. Be kind, embrace them, teach them, and make them feel welcome, at tournaments or on your own local courts.

You could very well be saving their life."

These stories offer insights as to how pickleball provides meaning, connection, healthy competition, and joy to its passionate devotees, regardless of age. Can you find echoes of your own life experience in these words? Take time to contemplate how pickleball has created a spark in your life. Think of the good souls you have encountered and look forward to seeing every week. If you are about to start or expand your own pickleball journey, consider how your life might open up to new possibilities.

Of course, we also love pickleball because it doesn't take itself too seriously. Whether your buddy completely whiffs an easy shot, or the ball you mishit floats into the corner for a winner, there's plenty to laugh about on the court. Every group has their own touching or funny stories that create camaraderie and a unique vibe. The ultimate crime in pickleball isn't stepping into the kitchen. . . it's not having a good time.

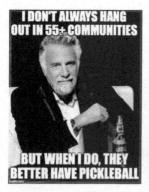 

And here are a couple of funny songs on YouTube that capture the goofiness of the game. Even if you've seen them before, they still bring a smile to your face...

I Wanna Dink With Somebody
The Pickleball Song

Every day you step on the court is an opportunity to re-imagine your athletic life and become part of a community that is supportive, inclusive, and fun. It may look like we're just hitting a plastic ball around, but dig a little deeper and you will discover why pickleball resonates so strongly with its devotees.

FINAL THOUGHTS

AT THE BEGINNING OF THIS BOOK, I promised to dig a little deeper and provide a more holistic view of pickleball, especially as it relates to the specific needs and desires of the senior player. Yes, on some level, it's just a game... but it really is so much more. It's an opportunity to compete, connect, and enjoy a healthier, more fulfilling life. If you're already a pickleball-addicted senior, I don't have to tell you how much fun this game can be. You get it! You certainly don't need to ponder any profound spiritual truths every time you're on the court—you just like to play. Yet sometimes it's illuminating to reflect on why this game has such a hold on us at a deeper level. We love the athletic and social aspects, but there are additional factors at play as well.

⊙ Purpose

As we age, we sometimes feel cast adrift. We may no longer have a job or need to raise a family. When we took up pickleball, we probably had no idea what we were getting into. Thankfully, many of us have found meaning and purpose in this little game and the people with whom we share the court. We may not be changing the world while we're on the court, but our days have structure, we get out and interact with others, form friendships, and have a reason to stay in shape and stay sharp.

We still have time to work, learn, and contribute to society, but we also have an outlet that challenges us to be better every day and allows us to play. As I mentioned at the outset, humans love to play. Play is a worthwhile purpose in and of itself. It is one of the joys of living that we're still not too old to savor.

⊙ Connection

You can never go too far astray if you expand your engagement with the world and those crazy, messy, wonderful people who frustrate and fulfill you. When you say "yes" to life, you come out a winner for having played the game no matter the outcome. Travel, play, laugh, compete, connect. Treasure the opportunity and your good fortune to be able to play a game in this often-unfair world. If that game is pickleball, I trust you will find the competitive leisure, physical/emotional health benefits, and human connection that continue to make this sport so popular.

⊙ Family

And finally, pickleball offers connection within families. It's great to see couples who play together or in separate games because of differences in ability. Each partner gets their "pickleball fix" and expands their social group. Parents and children play at home or at local clubs, and you can even find grandparents and grandkids sharing the court. It's one more valuable connection point for family togetherness, and a source of laughter and good-natured ribbing as well.

Even if your family doesn't play, you can create your own pickleball family from the friends you make on the court. As seniors, family and social connections keep us active and involved. Pickleball is the perfect pastime to bring us together, provide a fun challenge, and encourage us to be mentally, physically, and socially engaged.

When you look back at life through the misty lens of experience, you realize the greatest lesson is that your relationships ultimately have the most powerful effect on your happiness. Part of the magic of pickleball is the way it opens your world to new relationships. Nothing else in life compares to the highs, lows, and lessons learned from your interactions with others. (Not even the scores of your pickleball games...)

☺ Perspective

> Autumn is a second spring when
> every leaf is a flower.
>
> ~ *Albert Camus*

Happiness is all about savoring every day—and expressing who you are in every season of life. Autumn is more peaceful than the bursting of spring and the bustle of summer. The colors are richer. There is time to enjoy the harvest of the hard work that went before.

Your future may not be full of boundless possibilities as it was when you were young, but the autumn of life is often more suited to who you really are. To the extent possible, you have created a life that reflects your values. Ideally, you have surrounded yourself with good people who lift you up rather than competing with those around you for status, attention, and money.

Your motivations have naturally shifted from future-oriented goals to present moment joys—a walk in the forest, a sunset at the beach, playtime with a grandchild—without the distractions and demands of making a living or raising a family. You may not be able to run a marathon, but you can play pickleball, competing on *your* terms in an environment that suits *your* needs in this autumn of your life.

When you are on the court with friends, you are thrust into the present moment—you can't simultaneously worry and hit a winning volley. Your time on the court can be the perfect blend of challenge and fun, free from mental chatter and worldly concerns—fully absorbed in the joyfulness of play. And "play" keeps you young at heart. Pickleball is just a game... but so is life. Play it well.

Thanks for coming along. I hope you have learned a thing or two about playing better, healthier, and happier. I hope *your* pickleball story is a long, happy tale. Let's lead by example and show those youngsters how it's done.

"Carpe Dink-em"! Seize every day you get to play with your friends, no matter how "life-experienced" you are. See you on the courts!

Index
of Videos

- Video #1: Dinking Essentials: Low, Set, Push
- Video #2: Mastering the Third Shot Drop
- Video #3: The Reset: Stop, Drop, and Get Back on a Roll
- Video #4: Groundstrokes: Power and Consistency
- Video #5: The Volley: Keys to Dominance at the Net
- Video #6: All You Need is Lob
- Video #7: Footwork and Preparation: The Keys to Great Shot-Making
- Video #8: Deception and Aggression at the Kitchen

Videos can be viewed at
https://www.mikebranon.com/joy

Appendix 1: Resources

Books

These are my favorite books by category:

Instruction:

- **At the Line Pickleball**, Joe Baker

  The authoritative pickleball instruction book. Well researched and clearly written.

History:

- **History of Pickleball: More Than 50 Years of Fun!**, Youngren and Lucore

  Traces the uneven path of pickleball from backyard activity to booming sport.

  Also, check out Jennifer Lucore's website at www.all-pickleball.com for blogs and other resources. She was the first pickleball blogger (2012).

Everything Pickleball:

- **Pickleball For Dummies,** Various authors

  I know these authors and I was the Technical Editor for this book. They have put together a comprehensive, truly funny book in the whimsical spirit of the "Dummies" series.

Playing and Living Well:

- **Pickleball & The Art of Living,** Mike Branon

An exploration of getting the most out of life and your game. The author is handsome, brilliant, and humble.

Podcasts

There are several entertaining pickleball podcasts out there, but these are some of my favorites on which I have been a guest. Podcasts come and go, but even if some of these have been discontinued, you can check out archived episodes to find topics of interest.

- **Pickleball Fire,** Lynn Cherry

  Lynn has a background in sports psychology and her diverse guests touch on a wide array of subjects: a show with perspective that makes you think.

- **More or Less Pickleball,** Morgan Evans

Morgan is one of the game's great characters and owner of the most diabolical spin serve in the game. More laughs per minute than most podcasts.

- **Pickleball Problems,** Mark Renneson

  Mark is a Renaissance Picklehead. He coaches, commentates, and certifies pickleball coaches in his spare time. His style is both whimsical and analytical.

- **I Used to be Somebody,** Carl Landau

  This podcast has a pickleball flavor but it's mostly about enjoying "un-retirement". Quirky and fun!

Pickleball Tourism

- **Trespalapasbaja.com**

  Tres Palapas pickleball resort is located in Los Barriles, Mexico, one hour north of the San Jose del Cabo airport. It's where I go to get away and play. It's a great place to come as a single, couple, or group where you can interact with local players and enjoy the excellent onsite bar and café. (Their breakfasts and smoothies are to die for. . .) Your hosts, Paul and Sally Bland, have created a little slice of Mexico like it used to be— friendly, quiet, and featuring uncrowded beaches with delicious, reasonable dining options. And all the pickleball you can eat!

- **Thepuravidahouse.com**

This Costa Rica destination is an experiential treasure. The instruction is top-notch with resident coaches, Sylvain and Mani, plus an array of top pros hosting specialty weeks. Lodging is offered in luxurious homes in an exclusive, private community. Catering to groups of 12 or more, you can play and drill for 2-3 hours then luxuriate at the beach club, trek to nearby pristine beaches, or enjoy Costa Rica's amazing natural beauty. Book early as this place fills up fast.

- **Pickleballinthesun.com**

  Laura Vossberg Gainor has put together a site that caters to novices as well as experienced players who want to combine vacations and pickleball from coast to coast. As the owner of a pickleball marketing agency, she is well connected in the industry and is passionate about sharing her love for travel and pickleball.

- **Pickleballtrips.com**

  A family business dedicated to quality pickleball with an emphasis on the joy of travel for all ages. Domestic destinations as well as international trips to Europe, Asia, and the Caribbean.

- **Pickleballgetaways.com**

  Run by top pros, Dekel Bar and Ben Johns, pickleball intensive trips to exotic destinations in Mexico, the Caribbean, and Europe. Senior-friendly for players of all levels.

Pickleball Camps and Clinics

- **Engage Pickleball Camps**

  Engagepickleball.com
  Domestic and international sites
  Multiple clinics each month

- **LevelUp**

  Leveluppickleballcamps.com
  Domestic sites. Rated #1 in 2020 *Pickleball Magazine*
  Reader Survey
  Multiple clinics each month

- Nike Adult Pickleball Camps

  Ussportscamps.com
  Domestic sites

- Pickleballhelp.com

  Domestic and Caribbean sites
  Small group sizes

Clothing

These companies are owned by people I know who play pickleball and are passionate about the game. I'm proud to wear their gear.

- Civileapparel.com
- Phitwarrior.com
- Skybluepickleball.com

All Things Pickleball

- Pickleballcentral.com
- Totalpickleball.com
- Pickleballgalaxy.com
- Pickleballshopping.com

Appendix 2: Terms and Rules

Glossary

1. **Dink:** A soft shot hit on a bounce from the NVZ, intended to arc over the net and land within the opposing NVZ either straight across or diagonally crosscourt.
2. **Drop Shot:** The drop is a soft shot hit off a bounce from deep in the court, intended to land in the opponents' NVZ, preferably close to the net. It enables the hitting team to follow the shot to the NVZ line. It is the primary third shot, giving the serving team the opportunity to approach the net after the return of serve, but can also be effective any time the opponents are at the net.
3. **Volley:** A ball hit in the air before it bounces onto the court during a rally. It is often used when at the NVZ line to return a ball hit hard and low over the net.
4. **Lob:** A lofted shot that sends the ball high overhead and deep. Used to catch the opponent off guard or

force him/her back to the baseline (offensive). It can also be effective as a defensive shot to buy time to get into position for an offensive shot.

Basic Rules

- Pickleball is played either as doubles (two players per team) or singles—doubles is most common.
- The same size playing area and rules are used for both singles and doubles.

The Serve

- The server's arm must be moving in an upward arc when the ball is struck.
- Paddle contact with the ball must not be made above the waist level.
- The head of the paddle must not be above the highest part of the wrist at contact.
- A 'drop serve' is also permitted, in which case none of the elements above apply.
- At the time the ball is struck, the server's feet may not touch the court or outside the imaginary extension of the sideline or centerline, and at least one foot must be behind the baseline on the playing surface or the ground behind the baseline.
- The serve is made diagonally crosscourt and must land within the confines of the opposite diagonal court.

- Only one serve attempt is allowed per server.

Scoring

- Points are scored only by the serving team.
- Games are normally played to 11 points, win by 2.
- Tournament games may be to 15 or 21, win by 2.
- When the serving team's score is even (0, 2, 4, 6, 8, 10...), the player who was the first server in the game for that team will be in the right-side court when serving or receiving; when odd (1, 3, 5, 7, 9...), that player will be in the left-side court when serving or receiving.

Two-Bounce Rule

- When the ball is served, the receiving team must let it bounce before returning, and then the serving team must let it bounce before returning, thus two bounces.
- After the ball has bounced once in each team's court, both teams may either volley the ball (hit the ball before it bounces) or play it off a bounce (groundstroke).
- The two-bounce rule eliminates the serve and volley advantage and extends rallies.

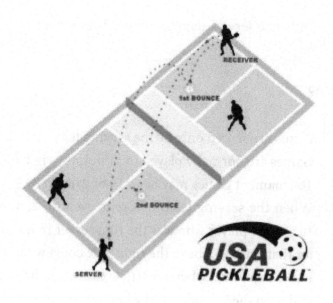

Non-Volley Zone

- The non-volley zone is the court area within seven feet on both sides of the net.
- Volleying is prohibited within the non-volley zone. This rule prevents players from executing smashes from a position within the zone.
- It is a fault if, when volleying a ball, the player steps on the non-volley zone, including the line and/or when the player's momentum causes them or anything they are wearing or carrying to touch the non-volley zone, including the associated lines.
- It is a fault if, after volleying, a player is carried by momentum into or touches the non-volley zone, even if the volleyed ball is declared dead before this happens.

- A player may legally be in the non-volley zone any time other than when volleying a ball.
- The non-volley zone is commonly referred to as "the kitchen."

Line Calls

- A ball contacting any part of any line, except the non-volley zone line on a serve, is considered "in."
- A serve contacting the non-volley zone line is short and a fault.

Faults

- A fault is any action that stops play because of a rule violation.
- A fault by the receiving team results in a point for the serving team.
- A fault by the serving team results in the server's loss of serve or side out.

Doubles Scoring

- Points are scored only on the serve; the receiving side cannot score a point.

- At the start of the game, the player on the right side (even court) serves to the diagonally opposite court.
- If a point is scored, the server moves to the left side (odd court) and serves to the diagonally opposite court.
- Players on the serving side continue to move from the right to left or left to right each time a point is scored.
- Players on the serving team do not alternate sides unless a point is scored. The receiving side never alternates sides.
- The first server continues to serve until the serving team loses a rally by committing a fault, then the serve passes to the second server on the team. [See * below for an exception.]
- When the second server loses the serve, the serve goes to the other team and the player on the right serves first. That pattern continues throughout the game.
- Calling the Score:
  - The score should be called as three numbers.
  - Proper sequence for calling the score is: server score, receiver score, then, for doubles only, the server number: 1 or 2.
  - To start a match, the score will be called as: zero – zero – two.*
- The server number (1 or 2) applies for that service turn only. Whoever is on the right side (depending on the score) when the team gets the serve back is the first server for that service turn only. The next time that the team gets the serve back, it might be the other player

that is on the right and is, therefore, the first server for that service turn only. Beginning players often mistakenly assume that the player keeps the same server number throughout the game.

- *First Server Exception: To minimize the advantage of being the first team to serve in the game, only one player, the one on the right side, gets to serve on the first service turn of the game. Since the serve goes to the other side when that player loses the serve, that player is designated as the second server. Therefore, at the start of the game, the score should be called, "0-0-2." The "2" indicates the second server and means that the serve goes to the other side when the serve is lost.

- When a team's score is even, the player who served first in that game must be on the right (even) side of the court, and on the left (odd) side when the score is odd. Or, expressed alternately, when the first server of that game is on the right side of the court, that team's score should be even. If this is not the case, then either the players are positioned on the wrong side of the court or the called score is inaccurate.

Usapickleball.org

Acknowledgments

Special thank you to those that helped make this book happen.

- Diane Branon, for your technical assistance and patience.
- Kara Williams: My pickleball video model and one of the nicest people you'll ever meet (no matter what Bob and Charles say).
- Rich Love, player, coach, and all-around good guy, for your input on "Dealing With Limitations".
- Andrew Montero and Chris Young for being my "highly paid" and fun video crew.
- Jennifer Lucore, Pickleball Hall of Famer, for your many contributions.
- Brett Noel, for sharing his "unbearably" cute teaching visual—Don't Feed the Bear!
- My invaluable Beta readers.
- My amazing students—thank you for your enthusiasm and hunger to learn. I appreciate our time together and your friendship.
- My fellow players, for all the good competition and great times.
- Special thanks to the good people who shared their stories: Paulette, Rick, Aubri, and Bill.

- Saundra and Bill Cima for sharing your tennis/pickleball court over the years and for more good years to come.
- David Wogahn at AuthorImprints for your guidance and support.

About the Author

Mike Branon is a non-professional pickleball player, but that hasn't stopped him from competing, coaching, and writing about pickleball. His varied background in business, sports, health, and psychology enables him to write with some credibility about how to succeed in any venture and enjoy the journey along the way. He lives in Carlsbad, California with his wife, Diane, and his trusty and occasionally obedient goldendoodle, Cabo.

Go to mikebranon.com for features, health tips, blogs, interviews, and strange musings about getting the most out of life and your game—or to contact Mike for coaching, speaking, or book signing events.

The following is an excerpt from my first book, *Pickleball & The Art of Living*. It explores how you can live your best life on and off the court, using pickleball as an example of how the right mindset and attitude enable you to get the most out of every day. It's less about instruction and more about living well. Hope you enjoy!

Scan the QR code below to view the book on my website, MikeBranon.com.

THE
ROAD MAP

NONE OF US ARRIVE AT ADULT-hood fully formed; we figure things out on the fly, buffeted by emotions and blown around by fate. Most of us are often too busy just getting by to pause and figure out better ways of living. And we'll never completely lose the insecurities of growing up and navigating life without a map.

If you want to be the driver of your life instead of being taken for a ride, you're going to need that map.

The map I'm offering you is this book. We're not going to speed down I-10 through Texas with eyes staring straight ahead. Think of this trip as an exploration, like poking along Route 66, A1A in Florida, or the Pacific Coast Highway, stopping at scenic lookouts and popping into quirky cafes. We will visit stops along the way to help you get the most out of your adventure. We will encounter roadblocks, find the detours, and Google Maps our way along the best routes. You will learn to navigate the world as your better self, discovering ways to maximize adventure, your backhand, and your well-being.

The goal of this journey is to fine-tune your mindset to

THE ROAD MAP

Assess Yourself

Before you can start the journey, you need to know where you are in the first place—be honest in your assessment. Seeing yourself clearly sets the stage for progress and fulfillment.

Develop a Growth Mindset

A growth mindset is a belief that success comes from effort, learning, and determination. Only when you believe in your power to change can you commit to the process.

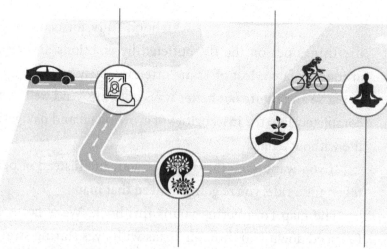

Understand the Interplay of Mind and Emotion

The unobserved mind is incapable of directing conscious change. Unobserved emotions can sabotage any rational plan. Understanding our mental and emotional selves and bringing them into unison is crucial to living well.

Engage Your Higher Self

Your body and mind truly thrive when they are guided by wisdom principles and imbued with passion and purpose.

get the most out of your game and your life—and have fun along the way.

So, let's get right to it—the motor's running. Let's look at the landmarks on your life map that can keep you headed in the right direction:

Create "Success Environments"

Consciously building virtuous habits provides the framework for success. Bad habits need to be replaced with new patterns that create healthy environments and yield positive results.

Live in the Present Moment

STOP! Notice life. It's amazing! We tend to get distracted—lost in thought, reliving the past and worrying about future scenarios. Be here now for that shot, that kiss, that tree, that breath... Now is the only time you truly have.

Develop Perspective and Self-Compassion

Striving without perspective can leave you dissatisfied no matter what you achieve in life. Self-compassion is the antidote to self-judgment. Try hard but accept that the destination is unknown and sometimes beyond your control. If your intentions and effort are true, you will have done your best.

If you follow this map, you will know where you are starting, understand where you are going, develop the right attitude and habits, and maintain the proper perspective to enjoy the journey. If you get lost at times, check back often with this road map to make sure you get where you want to go.

⊙ WE'RE ON OUR WAY

Even with a solid road map, the meaning of life is still an intimidating subject. It has been pondered by philosophers, poets, and priests. It has been studied by scientists, scholars, and statisticians. You can get lost and confused trying to figure out what it all means. But as the guy at the local taco stand says, "You're probably better off taking a small bite than trying to down the whole enchilada at once." So let's start by asking:

What is a *day* well lived?

This is perhaps the most fundamental question we can ask. Sometimes, when we look back at our day, we know that it has been a good one. We took time to enjoy, create, and be kind to ourselves and others. The stars aligned, things went well, and we lived with a sense of purpose. And, of course, a couple of hours of pickleball with friends just took it over the top.

Then there are the times we feel like it was just another day—spinning our wheels, going through the motions, getting little if anything done. What did happen didn't add up to much. We know we're alive but on days like these, it feels like time is just drifting by.

So what sets these two very different days apart? How can we get to a place where the "good days" happen far more often than those "bad days"? It all starts with our intention as we wake up.

Each day our eyes open, our senses stir, and the endless mental conversation begins. Taking inventory of any aches and pains, the "to do" list emerges as work, family, and chores vie for priority. We might experience a swirl of emotions on the spectrum from anticipation to dread. This moment of awakening sets the stage for the day. Do we rise with excitement and a sense of purpose? Or do we awaken gray and dull, resigned to just getting stuff done and making it through the day?

Intentional living enables us to cut through the haze and chaos. To put it in sports terms, it's approaching each day with a game plan. Living intentionally puts us on the offensive rather than the defensive. We develop the habit of acting with a purpose rather than reacting to problems and losing our way. Good days start to outnumber the bad ones more often as a positive attitude frames everything in a better light no matter what actually happens.

Sure, it's a lot easier to have a good attitude when our day consists of choosing what time to get a game in on Wednesday rather than one with a stressful deadline. There will be some days when you won't feel particularly happy as things go sideways. It may seem like every one of life's shots are hitting the tape and rolling over on your side of the net as you stand by helplessly. The art of living is to accept and abide. This difficult day will pass. And it will pass with less drama and consternation if you don't expect the universe to shower you with rainbows and chocolate chip cookies every day.

Whether good or bad, or more likely somewhere in between, a day well-lived demands intention and presence. We will explore this dynamic, identifying obstacles and developing virtuous habits that enable us to play and live our best.

⊛ THE BALANCING ACT

Even when we get what we want and life is smooth, restlessness eventually creeps in. Humans evolved to wander and wonder. Is there more to life than pickleball? (I know . . . *blasphemy.*)

We complain about the challenges in our lives but without challenge, life can become shallow and tedious. Don't get me wrong, relaxation and leisure time are essential parts of a balanced life. And sharing our lives with other unique humans is part of that balance, keeping us amused, comforted, and connected. The goal is to meet life's challenges, adversities, and opportunities with optimism and equanimity, engaged and alive. The key is to find the balance that suits *you;* to use your insights and experience to consciously fine-tune your life.

Once you have examined what makes a day well lived, you just need to repeat that process day after day until you end up with a *life* well lived. Seems simple enough, right? The problem is that we are human. We are easily distracted; our minds are constantly chattering away and our emotions and desires often lead us in different directions.

Implementing the concepts in this book has reduced the distracting noise in my life and given me clarity. I have applied these principles and habits to raise a happy family, find business success, explore new life paths, become a spiritual seeker and a decent pickleball player, and enjoy all that life has to offer.

I want to offer these discoveries to you as a gift, not a lecture. I definitely don't have all the answers but have stumbled upon some clues. Please take this book in the spirit in which it is intended: a desire to make your life—and pickleball—experience the best it can be.

⊛ CHILLIN' WITH THE LAUGHING BUDDHA

Your life path is complicated. You will have questions along the way:

- How do I become more aware and build a good life in the face of hardships and heartaches?
- How do I take wise action rather than rushing around in a state of reaction?
- What does it mean to feel alive and purposeful?
- Can I actually enjoy this process and have a few laughs along the way?

These are just some of the questions that have preoccupied philosophers and seekers throughout the ages—except maybe

145

the last one about laughter. Laughter sometimes gets cast aside in a serious search for universal truths, but as any Laughing Buddha will tell you: Enlightenment is even better when you're having a good time.

The original Laughing Buddha was a Buddhist Zen monk who lived in China more than a thousand years ago when there was no pickleball. (Can you imagine?) His name was Quieci but everyone called him "Budai." If he lived today his pals would probably call him Buddy, and he would be the one forwarding funny cat videos and doing online dance challenges. We will also call him Buddy throughout the rest of our ride because that's how he rolls when he's not at the monastery. He was devoted to the pursuit of wisdom but he loved to laugh and would remind everyone to enjoy life and be happy. Some would consider him to be out of line with the serious teachings and disciplined life of Buddhist monks but he played an important role—because what good is enlightenment if you can't share it with your pals after a game over a few beers or green teas?

Buddy loves him some pickleball.

Chances are that many of the big questions occasionally surface in *your* life but with the distractions of relationships, work, and pickleball games, these important issues are often pushed aside. This book is designed to help you focus on the essential wisdom that is the foundation for a life well lived. And then learn how to bring that wisdom into the world to create more peace and contentment in a way that is interesting, occasionally humorous, and easy to apply.

Speaking of humor, be forewarned that I have liberally sprinkled serious subjects with offbeat images and comments throughout this book. My inner Buddy just needs to get out and play sometimes. You'll get it soon enough but my message is pretty simple: Do your best, explore the wonders of life, but don't take things so seriously. After all, a life well lived should have more than its fair share of good times. When you can be mindful and ridiculous at the same time you're doing it right.

YOUR STORY, MY STORY

A FRIEND OF MINE IN THE BOOK business warned me that getting someone to read a book can be like inviting them to share an elevator with you, pushing the "STOP" button, and talking at them for ten hours. You'll probably want to get to know me better before hopping in and hoping for the best. While I hope my life story gives you some clues as to what has shaped my perspective and inspired me to share what I have learned with you, this book is really about *your* story.

Each one of us is the writer, director, and actor of our life stories. The mystery is that we don't know how it will all turn out. The challenge is to live well no matter what plot twists await us. As you read, stop and reflect on the journey you have been on and the road ahead. See if the pages to come hold any clues as to how to actively direct you[...] circumstances do the job for you.

Today I'm retired, living a blessed lif[...] a wonderful woman. (Despite what it seems like, I'm not married to pickle-ball. Pickleball and I spend a LOT of time together but I still see tennis and golf on the side.) I have two great kids and a little grandson. If you'll indulge me, I want to tell you the story of how I got here so you can better know why I am passionate about the messages I want to share.

Rowan Michael (because pictures of grandkids are always a good thing).

🏓 FAMILY: WHERE OUR STORIES BEGIN

My personal journey to finding my enough is best seen through the prism of my family. My dad was in the Navy and my mom was a nurse. Early on, they arrived at a new tour of duty in North Carolina in a Ford station wagon with $1.37 to their name. My Dad had to trade the spare tire of the car for a night in a seedy motel upon reaching Camp Lejeune.

My father is a guy you would not want to mess with. He was often embedded with the Marines in some pretty rough spots and he was known as an excellent marksman. As I got older, I heard many harrowing stories from tough military guys who knew and deferred to him; those stories would make the hair stand up on the back of your neck. But he was always a caring father to my brothers and me, spending any free time he had with us. We bounced around military bases—Key West, the Washington D.C. area, and both sides of the Panama Canal zone. Our four years in Panama were particularly memorable as we spent our time in the jungle with machetes or out on the ocean sailing and swimming with sharks and around pirate wrecks along the rugged coast.

The funny thing is, as my dad admits, my mom is probably tougher than he is. She had to raise three wolves masquerading as boys, oftentimes for long stretches by herself while my dad was away. She had plenty of practice—she grew up poor in a difficult situation where she was the caretaker of her younger siblings. She once stopped a local crime spree during our time in Panama by attacking a canoe full of bandits with her tennis racket as they attempted to scale the seawall by our living quarters. They never came back. Even now, in her eighties, I have yet to see her take more than she gives in any aspect of her life.

The Branon boys—I'm the one with my pet barracuda, Barry (circa 1972).

My younger brothers were no shrinking violets either. They grew into the size of linebackers and made their living with their hands and guile, sometimes on the wrong side of the law. My youngest brother had movie-star looks, charisma, and an appetite for power. Unfortunately, he never found his "enough" and couldn't stop even when he could afford to do so. In spite of his good qualities and his devotion to his friends and son (who was tragically murdered), he is doing life in prison. My middle brother is the only guy I know who may be as tough as my youngest brother. He is funny as hell, cares deeply for animals, but has little patience with humankind. Like my dad, he is a great ally and a terrible enemy.

There was never a lot of open affection in our family, but there was a lot of laughter and we all knew we had each other's backs. Having such tough, hard-working parents instilled a drive in me that has never completely gone away. I was the white sheep of the family. I excelled at school and loved music and sports. I couldn't bear to lose at anything and finally came to realize that I was driven in part by a desire to never let my parents down. My dad sensed this, and in spite of his success as a military officer and, later, an accomplished novelist, he took every opportunity to tell self-deprecating stories about himself. Neither he nor my mom ever put the least amount of pressure on me, knowing that there was plenty of that inside of me already.

After a successful academic career, I hit a wall in the job market, utterly failing for the first time. I made ends meet by working in a convenience store and refereeing basketball part-time. Eventually I got married and found a somewhat decent job working almost entirely on commission, but I was never really okay with just being okay. I was happy enough but was unduly hard on myself and sometimes others.

My job became less fulfilling as time went on. I had been working for a steel construction company for eight years and had plateaued as far as opportunity and challenge. My marriage was also falling apart. The only thing that kept us together was momentum and our young daughter. Divorce finally became inevitable and I found myself on my own in a small rented room in a stranger's house. I felt the sting of failure more acutely than ever. Fortunately, through trial and error, wrong turns and confusion, I eventually figured something out:

A life well lived is a celebration of who you are. It is not belittling yourself on some level for who you are not.

Sitting on the floor with my two-year-old daughter in that room, I finally had time to let that discovery sink in. The joy of just being with my daughter and seeing the curiosity and optimism in her made my entire surroundings and life situation fade into the background. I tried to put all the noise and doubt swirling around in my head aside and reacquainted myself with living in the moment, something kids do naturally. Only then was I able to rebuild my life from scratch.

Armed with this healthier mindset, I transitioned into a new relationship with someone I had known for years and who had a young son of her own. As John Madden used to say, "BOOM," instant family! I also began to look at my career and explore ways to forge my own path. I had developed ideas about what my own company might look like and established relationships that would allow me to hit the ground running. I just had to pull the trigger, but child support and a new mortgage payment left me fearful of starting from scratch with no guaranteed paycheck.

Finally, I mustered the courage to make the move. I decided to concentrate on the self-storage construction market, seeing a niche opportunity in a relatively new industry. I attacked the new venture with energy and determination and opened my own construction business in my dining room. Through hard work, good coworkers, and a lot of luck, I was on my way to a life I never knew I could have.

After six years, the company had grown to become one of the leaders in the industry. But the constant stress and time away from the kids had begun to wear on me. One day, as I was taking the train back home along the Pacific coast after another grueling week, I gazed wearily at the crashing waves and the horizon beyond. I suddenly realized that the noise I had worked so hard to push aside had found its way back into my head. I had spent the last seven years so focused on the grind that I hadn't even noticed.

That train ride home allowed me the time to reassess my journey and truly see the opportunity before me. I once had the fortitude to start my own business and now I needed to summon that same conviction to leave safe harbor and head out toward the horizon of new and uncertain possibilities. I stepped back and my staff stepped up and did fine without me. A new chapter had begun and I was excited to see how the story would unfold.

⊙ MY SECOND ACT

After I left the company, I spent the next year building my family's new home in the San Diego area. I was looking for a new challenge and building a home turned out to be the perfect transition to the next phase of my life.

I had found a level of peace and gratitude, but still felt compelled to take on new challenges that were appropriate to my state of mind. I went to massage school to learn skills that would help my aching body and enable me to help others. My wife and I traveled like never before, enjoying adventures with our kids and friends. I devoted myself to the nonprofit sector, serving on boards and working on special projects. Most importantly, I embarked on a spiritual journey that opened my eyes to new ways of seeing things. For the first time, I actively explored a world I never seemed to have time for in the past. I devoured great books and joined groups to feed the spiritual self that I had been too busy to fully examine.

It was a revelation—I was able to find new ways of being that added immeasurably to my experience of life. I was still engaged with creating and exploring, but possessed with a newfound feeling of acceptance and serenity.

As my fourth and fifth decades flew by, my kids moved out and became independent. My hair went on vacation without me and never came back. (I hope it's having fun somewhere.) Wrinkles have appeared and arthritis is knocking on the door, but I love my wife, family, and friends. I continue to learn and seek truth in a post-truth world. I play pickleball, sip my bourbon, try to savor every day and appreciate the many good people I have encountered along the way.

I have had the privilege of working with numerous charities and have traveled at home and abroad to provide rebuilding efforts after natural disasters and healthcare to those in need. I have served on the board and taught world religions and psychology at a school that values holistic education in the best sense. I have supported and overseen leadership programs for young women and bereavement counseling for those who have lost a loved one. With these programs, I've seen families moving back into their once destroyed homes, somebody's health or vision restored, and was able to hug a mother or child who had been given a new chance to cope with their own cruel luck—these are the satisfying moments when compassion meets action. I am inspired by those who do much more than me to ease suffering and bring light back into the eyes of those whose dreams have dimmed.

But this is my journey. You have a completely different life path to navigate. Your dreams will differ from mine. But at its core, your journey has the same purpose—to learn how to end up with a life well lived. I'm sharing what worked for me in the hopes it can make your pickleball and life experience more enjoyable and meaningful too.

PROGRESS, NOT PERFECTION

THE PURSUIT OF PERFECTION CAN be a noble quest, but when perfection becomes an obsession, you may become blind to learning experiences and joyful moments along the way. You can be left feeling disillusioned by your inability to reach an unrealistic goal.

When you expect perfection from others, you are setting them up for failure as well. In spite of what Jerry Maguire says, *"You . . . complete me"* is a pretty hard standard to live up to. But, *"You . . . are a valued complement to me and I appreciate you for who you are as we both seek to navigate life together and as individuals. How does Mexican food sound tonight?"* probably wouldn't have been as catchy. And Renée Zellweger would have nodded off halfway through his monologue.

My unrealistic relationship with perfection had been holding me back. Getting divorced woke me up. Walking away from my business set me free. It took years to learn that trying to be perfect was a fool's game. I had to realize that divorce wasn't giving up—it was waking up to reality. The "perfect husband" image I had been trying to cultivate (and failing to reach) was holding me back from real progress in my life. And the outsized image of the successful businessman was an illusion as well; it was just part of who I was.

If I had remained a prisoner to the status quo and been afraid to change, my life wouldn't have turned out so well, and I never would have known any different.

By all means, take on the challenge of living well. But give yourself a break too. We're human, and every one of us is a work in progress. And the world we live in is unpredictable. There's no need to immediately jump ship when things aren't going as planned. By all means, stick with a good spouse or a rewarding job; they don't have to be perfect any more than you do. But don't be afraid to turn the car around when you see the "Dead End" sign in front of you.

Expecting perfection on the court is a guaranteed method for having a bad time too. Give yourself a break. And by all means, give your pickleball partner a break too. Nothing is less attractive in a partner than eye rolls, grunts of disapproval, or heavy sighs. They didn't show up to try to miss shots and ruin your day. Enjoy the process and face challenges with optimism, humility, and courage. Treasure the little victories and savor the progress you are making.

A day well lived or a game well played is one in which you have consciously given the best version of yourself, no matter what that is.

So why should you listen to me? I don't pretend to have invented a groundbreaking system that unlocks the secrets of the universe in a catchy ten-step program. I have no agenda to upsell you with my *Unleash Your Inner Pickleball Goddess* or *Pickle Your Way to a Flatter Stomach* sequels.

Am I qualified through education or profession to pontificate on the meaning of life? Um . . . no. I'm not a doctor nor do I play one on TV. As I mentioned earlier, my career and life path have taken a lot of twists and turns. I worked at McDonalds, in a factory, managed retail stores, ran my own construction company; was certified as a massage therapist, bereavement facilitator, and bartender; helped oversee nonprofits; taught high school; and co-owned a micro-brewery. And that's just a partial list of my job history. Talk about ADD . . .

However, I've also spent a lot of time reading, observing, and practicing—in other words, gathering information, seeing what works for me, and applying it to real-life situations. I hope this book will save you from the wrong turns that I have made and the time I've wasted as a result. I want to offer you a Whitman's Sampler of useful nuggets (because life is like a box of chocolates) that inspire you to find out what makes life delicious for you.

We all have different views, experiences, and opinions about what makes a good life. Ideally, we could sit down, share ideas, and figure it out together over a few beers like I do with my friends. But now, after all the time we've spent together, I feel like you and I have gotten pretty close already. You're feeling it too? Awww . . . thanks. So let's do this.

⊛ THE ROAD AHEAD

If you feel like more happiness and a more enjoyable pickleball experience might be a good thing, here's where I want to take you in the following pages:

First, we will take a look at why we play this game. If you're new to pickleball, perhaps this section will pique your curiosity and encourage you to pick up a paddle and join in the fun. And even if you're a grizzled veteran maybe you will get something out of my perspectives on the game.

Then we will explore ways to live better and achieve a greater awareness that is in alignment with your legitimate needs and desires. We will dig deep to examine the roadblocks that conspire to keep you from thriving and explore insights to inspire you to find greater meaning and contentment on and off the court. Along the way, we will discuss everything from meditation to dinking, spirituality to strategy, emotional intelligence to just having a good time. The idea is to align yourself with what is true and meaningful to you as you navigate an unpredictable world filled with crazy people like us.

Many of you have already pretty much found the life

balance you want. Take any advice in the spirit it is given . . . from a desire to help. I hope you enjoy the ride. If not, I hope the size of the book is just right for sticking under one of the legs on your Christmas tree stand. That way at least I'll have contributed to a sense of balance in your life one way or the other.

You may notice that I will be speaking directly to you in the chapters to come. I don't want to deliver a lecture; I prefer a conversation. Granted, it's going to be somewhat one-sided, but if I start to drone on you can just shut the book and go for a walk. I won't mind. And your dog will be thrilled. In fact, I would prefer you read this book in small chunks and occasionally contemplate what you have read instead of steaming ahead at full speed. Part of my message is to pause and take notice, to live mindfully and become aware of the cruise control that may be taking you to destinations you don't really want to visit. In fact, throughout the book I will gently remind you to stop and consider something that has, in my opinion, earned a contemplative pause. Since I'm a dog person, I will insert a pause (paws) symbol after a thought that invites contemplation, invoking the footprint of one of my favorite dogs ever, Crash. May he always chase rabbits but refuse to hurt them.

WARNING!

There's a little bit of a self-help
vibe in this book.

I have to admit that I back away a little bit when I hear the term "self-help." The genre has produced and continues to put out worthwhile information in a sincere attempt to help people live their best lives and make the world a better place. Many of these books seek to explore crucial philosophical questions in a way that makes deep truths more accessible and user-friendly. But sometimes, as the following real book titles (with my side notes) make clear, the self-help train goes off the rails.

The Beginner's Guide to Sex in the Afterlife

(Make sure to pay particular attention to the halo. It will make her wings flutter.)

Why Cats Paint

(Because they stepped in paint?)

How to Live with a Pregnant Wife

(Step 1: Don't let her see you reading this book.)

You're Sharp Enough to Be Your Own Surgeon

(Uh, no. You're not. Put down the knife.)

Natural Bust Enlargement with Total Mind Power

(Written by a man. So remember, when he's staring at your cleavage, he's just trying to help.)

How People Who Don't Know They're Dead Attach Themselves to Innocent Bystanders and What to Do About It

(Okay. That actually sounds useful.)

If any of those titles make you want to put down this book and explore something *really* interesting, I get it. Otherwise I invite you to come along and see if my twisted version of pickleball self-help is more arousing than sex in the afterlife. Besides, you'll have a lot of time for that later.

⚙ OUR YELLOW BRICK ROAD

In *The Wizard of Oz*, each of the main characters eventually comes to realize that they already had what they were searching for—a brain, a heart, courage, a home. The Yellow Brick Road is literally *our* life path. The wicked witch and flying monkeys (I'm still a little scarred by them) are the internal and external forces fighting to keep our heroes from finding out that their true selves were already enough. They simply had to discover what lay hidden from them.

Buddy tells me there is a Buddhist concept that we are all gems. We just need to be polished through right mind, action, and thought to let our true nature shine. So again, here is the (yellow brick) road before us . . .

I don't care much for the belief that we are innately sinful and bad in some way. This book is intended to serve as a guide to help you find your way home to the good already within you. We will travel the path together to uncover our best selves and enjoy the game we love. You will learn to deal with the flying monkeys in your brain that keep you from getting the most out of your abilities. And finally, you will learn to fine-tune your experience to achieve a balance that suits you and makes those around you happy you showed up on the court and in their lives. It really is that simple . . . and that hard.

Now let's kick some Wicked Witch butt.

PICKLEBALL& THE ART OF LIVING

Pickleball & The Art of Living is available in eBook and paperback formats. Order on Amazon, or visit MikeBranon.com to get a signed, dedicated copy from me.

Scan the QR code below to view the book on my website.